PORTFOLIO
STRATEGIES FOR GROWTH

Atanu Ghosh is a visiting professor of business policy at IIM Ahmedabad, and professor at the School of Management, IIT Bombay. He teaches and researches in the areas of strategy, leadership and marketing. He has over eighteen years of experience in various corporate organizations. He is currently the dean, alumni and external relationships, at IIMA.

INDIA'S BESTSELLING BUSINESS BOOKS SERIES

IIM
AHMEDABAD
BUSINESS BOOKS

STRATEGIES
FOR GROWTH

Help Your Business Move Up the Ladder

ATANU GHOSH

PORTFOLIO
PENGUIN

An imprint of Penguin Random House

PORTFOLIO

USA | Canada | UK | Ireland | Australia
New Zealand | India | South Africa | China | Singapore

Portfolio is part of the Penguin Random House group of companies
whose addresses can be found at global.penguinrandomhouse.com

Published by Penguin Random House India Pvt. Ltd
4th Floor, Capital Tower 1, MG Road,
Gurugram 122 002, Haryana, India

Penguin
Random House
India

First published in Random Business by Random House India 2010
Published by Penguin Random House India 2016
Published in Portfolio by Penguin Random House India 2018

ISBN 9788184001488

Printed at Manipal Technologies Limited, India

www.penguin.co.in

MIX
Paper | Supporting
responsible forestry
FSC® C043100

This is a legitimate digitally printed version of the book and therefore might not
have certain extra finishing on the cover.

*To my wife Oliva,
daughter Anulipi,
and all family members
and
my teachers, friends, colleagues, and well-wishers
all over the world*

CONTENTS

CONTENTS

Foreword

Dear Reader,

The book you are holding is one of the books from the IIMA Business Books series published in collaboration with Random House to disseminate knowledge to executives in a manner that brings them up to date in different fields of management. The books are written by authors who have rich experience of teaching executives from a diverse set of organizations. Written in a conversational style with numerous illustrations from the world of experience, you will find the books useful in your work life. The references cited in the books provide you with ready information on where to look for more detailed information on specific topics and concepts. I am certain you will enjoy reading the book. Write to us suggesting topics that you will like being covered in the books that are to be published under the series in the future.

Samir K. Barua
Director
IIM Ahmedabad

Introduction

All organizations aim to follow a trajectory of uninterrupted growth, irrespective of their nature. It doesn't matter if an organization is big or small, family or professionally managed, owned by private investors or public, or whether it's manufacturing or service based. That said, the ways of attaining growth are not simple. Depending on a variety of factors—from the size of the organization, its available resources, current trends in the business environment, the aptitude of its staff or the product or service being sold—growth can take many forms and be achieved through various means. Certain organizations may be in a position where an initiative such as market penetration is the best option, whereas some larger companies may benefit most by a merger or even the takeover of another company. As you will see, each decision must be taken carefully, after much research and deliberation and based on what makes sense logically.

This book begins with an understanding of the objectives for pursuing growth strategies, contextual differences between different routes with real examples of how companies have been successful in their bids to grow. Also stressed and explained are the challenges various types of organizations must face to maintain their profitability as they grow bigger. All too often organizations rest on their laurels when they reach a certain size, but as things get more complicated, it is all the more important to be vigilant and also stay creative—both with current products and services as well as in developing new ones.

This book focuses on various strategies that companies can adopt to achieve sustainable and profitable growth. It is important to realize that to do so, it is imperative to understand the organizational or management challenges that may arise in this context. When a certain growth strategy is implemented, a few challenges are thrown up. If the challenges, both faced when the venture is in progress as also those that appear after the strategy has proven to be successful, are not understood then an organization could find itself in big trouble. This may happen even if their initial plans are successful.

Broadly speaking, companies can follow several different avenues for achieving profitable and sustainable growth, the most important of which have chapters dedicated to these. Scenarios faced by virtually any company wishing to grow are described, along with specific examples, such as how a scooter company fought to maintain its image, or how McDonald's turned itself around after a slump and kept its spot as one of the most recognizable brands in the world.

An organization needs to carefully choose the area of their growth. Most markets are very fickle, and one misstep could jeopardize an entire undertaking. Management needs to be well prepared and well informed about the business environment in question before thinking about which area they'd like to grow, and once that is achieved, there is the matter of strategizing how best to introduce their product or service into a market successfully. This brings in a whole new set of variables. When the growth strategy is underway, as mentioned above, to be able to sustain the new product or service in the market requires constant monitoring, and if need be, tweaking in a number of areas,

- adjustments to the product or service itself,
- where the product or service is sold,
- an advertising campaign, or
- where advertisements are placed.

Constant feedback is crucial. The choice to expand a business is not an easy one, and not one for the faint hearted or half-committed. Diversification, for example, is a multi-faceted undertaking that requires manpower at various levels that will be able to identify the best way to use an organization's resources as well as to be able to see gaps in both markets and in the company's capabilities.

For companies at a higher level, growth can be achieved through methods such as disruptive innovation. But to do that, a product or service must be seen as powerful enough to enter a market which already has a few successful players. The organization must have the resources to back this kind of move, which can prove costly in its bid for a place in a crowded marketplace.

Many readers may be managers themselves at various points in their careers, working at companies with very different assets. It is hoped that this book will prove useful to managers from all types of business, and appeal to young, aspiring managers, and the layman as well—after all, no matter what level, with so many factors and choices to be made, it's always good to have some experienced advice.

This book is intended to sensitize the reader to all areas and modes they may encounter when they decide to expand their business. Hopefully in more than a few instances, examples and advice in this book will be what readers need to hear at the right time to make an informed, intelligent decision about how to do so.

This book seeks to address all the concerns above and more. For in today's marketplace, strategies for growth are more important for success than ever before. Globalization has brought world markets, products, and services to our door. It is in these pages that we will look at how to make the best of current and coming trends in Indian business practice.

1

Growth through Market Penetration

INTRODUCTION

Among the several options available for an organization to grow in a given business, this chapter will discuss the option of market penetration, which involves the least risk and the deployment of minimal resources. We will examine tools like the Market Opportunity Index and the Sustainable Competitive Advantage Index, both of which decision makers should consult before deciding whether or not they should look for growth in existing markets using existing products. The Market Opportunity Index serves as a tool to evaluate the potential and scope of a business's external environment. On the other hand, the Sustainable Competitive Advantage Index can help evaluate the strengths and weakness of an organization which can drive or hinder sustainable growth of the organization. Using the indices, decision makers can identify which opportunities to target for growth, find gaps within the organization which need to be plugged to achieve growth, or further leverage existing strengths. Thereafter, the discussion moves on to the option of niche versus mass marketing and their advantages and disadvantages. Finally, we move on to strategic implications of market share and conclude with three illustrations of market penetration initiatives by a market leader, a new player in a saturated market, and a niche player.

MARKET PENETRATION—ONE STRATEGIC GROWTH OPTION

Organizations that desire to survive in the long run must keep growing. There are multiple options that decision makers may opt for when they evaluate the options available for reaching their potential. Besides market penetration, other strategic options are product development, market development, and diversification, which will be discussed in subsequent chapters. Market penetration refers to growing with existing products in existing markets. This can be achieved by attracting new users in existing markets, by attracting and gaining competitors' customers, and by influencing current consumers to use more of the organization's product/service.

Usage can be increased by increasing the quantity or frequency of consumption. Several options can be exercised for the purpose. One may change the packaging design, that is, increase the package size, or some other innovation in the design to increase the amount of consumption per usage occasion. The usage of impulse products such as chocolates or snacks can be increased by increased availability and increased visibility at the purchase point.

Another option is to publicize new usage occasions so that the overall usage quantity of the product increases. The marketing communication can be designed aiming at communicating to the consumers the appropriateness and benefits of using the brand more frequently in new or existing occasions, and/or remind the consumers regularly to use the organization's product/service as featured in communications (advertisements).

Another possible opportunity to increase frequency of consumption arises when consumers perceive and use the product beyond its actual lifespan.[1] For many products with short lifespans, consumers may not replace the product when they should because of overestimating the productive life of the product. In such situations, one useful strategy could be linking the replacement of a product to a specific occasion, such as Holi, Diwali, or any other festival. Another useful strategy used by some organizations is to tag a usage meter with the product, such as the blue stripe on a Gillette Mach3 cartridge, which fades after repeated use and, when gone, prompts the user to change the cartridge.

MARKET OPPORTUNITY INDEX AND SUSTAINABLE COMPETITIVE ADVANTAGE INDEX

When the aim is to grow in existing markets, it is essential to regularly monitor the attractiveness of the market and the organization's relative competitive strength in order to grow in that market with the existing product range. That's where the Market Opportunity Index and the Sustainable Competitive Advantage Index come in.[2] The Market Opportunity Index is composed of three factors: a) market forces, b) competitive rivalry, and c) access to customers. Each of these factors is composed of three sub-factors. The market force factor is composed of market size, market growth rate, and buyer power. Competitive rivalry is composed of price rivalry, ease of entry, and substitutes available. Access to the customer is composed of customer familiarity, channel access, and sales force capabilities. Each of these sub-factors is to be assigned a score based on the attractiveness rating scale (Figure 1.1). Each of these factors and subsequent sub-factors are assigned a relative importance, such that the relative importance percentage of a factor's three sub-factors adds up to

100 percent. Similarly, the relative importance percentage of the three factors should also add up to 100 percent.

FIGURE 1.1: ATTRACTIVENESS RATING SCALE

Extremely unattractive	Unattractive	Moderately unattractive	Moderately attractive	Attractive	Extremely attractive
0	20	40	60	80	100

The Market Opportunity Index score is attained using the formula below.

Market Opportunity Index = *Market Forces Total Score x Relative Weight of Market Forces + Competitive Rivalry Total Score x Relative Weight of Competitive Rivalry + Access to Customers Total Score x Relative Weight of Access to Customers*

The Market Opportunity Index gives us an insight on an external environment's attractiveness. But there is not much that one can do about the external environment. If the environment is too hostile, the organization may decide to wrap up operations in that market or segment. Similarly, a market with a higher attractiveness index score may give confidence for higher investment. One can estimate the potential for growth or design strategy for growth in existing markets with an existing portfolio of products based on the organization's competitive advantage. Sustainable competitive advantage index is composed of three factors: a) product or service differentiation advantage, b) cost competitiveness and c) marketing strength. Each of these is composed of three sub-factors. Differentiation advantage is composed of product quality, service quality, and brand image. Cost advantage is composed of cost per unit, transaction cost, and marketing expenses. Marketing advantage is composed of market share, brand awareness, and distribution strength.

To express an organization's competitive advantage, use the following formula.

Sustainable Competitive Advantage Index = *(Product/Service Differentiation Advantage Total Score × Relative Weight of Product/ Service Differentiation Advantage) + (Cost Competitiveness Total Score × Relative Importance of Cost Competitiveness) + (Marketing Strength Total × Relative Weight of Marketing Strength)*

The Market Opportunity Index indicates opportunities or threats in the external environment. The Sustainable Competitive Advantage Index indicates an organization's strengths and weaknesses, that is, the capability of the organization to tap opportunities or tackle the threats in the environment to attain sustainable growth.

To gain market share it is important that organizations have a competitive advantage. The general perception is that an organization with first-mover advantage, that is, one which first introduces a product into the market, gains competitive advantage and thereby gains higher market share. Even as a second mover, an organization can gain first-mover competitive advantages in several ways. The organization can refine the imperfections in innovations pioneered by the competitor, or could focus on new services, or introduce variations in product delivery and gain competitive advantage. Products usually have both tangible and intangible benefits. Late movers that do not have much scope to gain competitive advantage may attempt to differentiate intangible service dimensions. If there is not much scope to differentiate on the core product, one may focus on its peripheral benefits. There is also significant scope to differentiate on how the organization communicates its message, or whether it is able to lead the market in price changes, or how accessible its products are for the consumers. Each of these options is illustrated in examples below.

Aircel (a late mover in a highly competitive telecom market) used an innovative idea for promotion. It hung rescue boats on billboards before the monsoon which could be used in case the area was flooded. Once the area actually did flood, it was these boats which rescued several stranded people long before any other rescue operation could be initiated. The scale of publicity and thereby the mindshare created by this campaign helped it gain market share. Similarly, Tata Docomo was a late entrant in the extremely competitive telecom market.

Tata Docomo is a joint venture between Tata Teleservices and Japan's Docomo. It introduced 1 paisa per second pricing for local as well as long distance calls. Prior to this the charges were per minute, which meant that even if the customer called for one or two seconds one had to pay for the entire minute. This offer proved to be a market-leading move and helped Tata Docomo immensely in penetrating the market and gaining market share from competitors.

One of the major strengths on which ITC gained market share in the potato chips and finger snacks category was distribution. When ITC's Bingo was introduced, Lays was ruling the market along with several other local players. ITC leveraged its presence and relationships in small kiosks to increase the visibility of Bingo.

Managers must recognize that it's not only the introduction of a product that gives first-mover advantage. There are several other areas where first-mover advantages can be found and can be leveraged upon if one is vigilant and innovative.

NICHE VERSUS MASS MARKETING

Niche marketing is to target a narrowly defined customer group in search of a specific mix of benefits, usually identified by dividing segments into sub-segments.[3] Characteristics of an attractive niche market are as follows:

▶ Customers have a specific set of needs
▶ Customers are ready to pay a premium for a product/service if it satisfies their needs
▶ Niche (marketer) would have comparatively much less competition
▶ Niche marketer gains advantages through specialization
▶ Niche market has enough size, profit, and growth potential for an organization to grow sustainably

Several companies in India have niche products in their portfolio. Crack by Paras Pharmaceuticals, Ezee from Godrej, and Itchguard are such examples. Crack is an ointment for cracked heels targeted at women. Itchguard is an ointment which protects against itching. Ezee is a liquid detergent sold specifically for washing woollen clothes. There are several television channels serving niche markets such as Aastha, which features religious and spiritual programmes serving the needs of special-interest viewers.

Niche marketers like organic or natural food providers usually charge a premium price for their products, and customers are willing to pay. There is little or no competition in such a niche market, which would make a price war unlikely. With time, as efficiency increases, niche markets become profitable with lucrative growth potential. Himalaya Herbal Healthcare, which focuses on ayurvedic medicines and natural health supplements, serves a growing niche market.

Globalization has provided niche marketers even higher potential for substantial growth as they spread their operations beyond their national boundaries. Tetra Food, which supplies food for feeding tropical aquarium fish, caters to 80 percent of the market. The low cost of setting up an Internet business has also allowed the growth of many niche businesses. There are several matrimonial sites, namely, www.bharatmatrimony.com and www.jeevansaathi.com which cater to specific demand and are performing well. Many times an organization in the early phase of its life cycle operates as a local niche player, and then subsequently diversifies into other geographic territories—The Body Shop, for example. Niche players are usually dedicated to their customers, offer customized service, intimate relationships, and on-time delivery.

Contrary to niche marketers, mass marketers target a wider range of customers and the focus is on gaining scale and leveraging previous gains. Mass marketers engage in mass production, mass promotion, and mass distribution. They operate with undifferentiated products/services with a focus on attaining overall cost leadership, and making the products available and accessible at all possible points of sale. Mavalli Tiffin Room (commonly known as MTR) is a food-related enterprise which serves a common breakfast and lunch menu. Similarly, the thali services that deliver a set lunch and dinner menu in many parts of India can be considered a mass service. Even the 'dabbawala' service in Mumbai is a mass service. Several commodities such as rice, sugar, and other grocery items are also non differentiated mass products.

One may notice a difference in organizational structure between mass marketers and niche marketers. Mass marketing organizations have a more centralized structure with low flexibility. Niche marketing organizations are characterized by decentralized structures with strategic business units if the organization is large; if small, there is a focus on one part of the market.

STRATEGIC IMPLICATIONS OF MARKET SHARE

Sales figures do not always project the true picture of an organization's performance relative to its competitors. Changes in sales figures may occur due to changes in market size or other environmental conditions. The performance of an organization can be more appropriately measured by the proportion of the market that the organization is able to capture, and this proportion is referred to as 'market share'. A firm's/product's/category's market share can be calculated as the ratio of the firm's/product's/category's sales versus total market sales. The sales revenue may be calculated on a value basis (that is, sales price × volume) or on a unit basis (number of units sold or number of customers served). While the revenue figures of an organization are readily available, total market sales are comparatively difficult to determine. The usual source of market figures are trade associations and market research firms such as AC Nielson or IMRB.

The reasons organizations seek to gain market share are multi-fold. Higher market share results in gaining economies of scale and thus facilitates developing cost advantages. In a highly competitive market, cost advantage frees up resources for delivering better services, launching new products, reducing prices, and increasing budgets for advertising and promotions; all of which, if executed appropriately likely to translate into further growth. Higher market share also helps in reputation building and increased visibility at the point of sale. Increase in market share also increases bargaining power, which gives an advantage in negotiations with suppliers and channel members.

The key drivers of a product's market share are share of preference, share of voice, and share of distribution. A product's market share can also be considered to have arisen from share of preference, share of voice, and share of distribution. These factors can be increased through proper price design, promotion, and distribution strategies. Share of preference is the percentage of a market's share of customers who prefer an organization's product over the competition. This can be increased through changes in pricing and promotional strategies. Share of voice is a brand's or portfolio of brands' advertising costs expressed as a percentage of a defined total market or market segment's advertising expenses in a given time period, which can be increased by increasing advertising expenditures. Share of distribution is the percentage of space a product occupies out of total space available for that category at points of sale. Share of distribution can be increased by building and sharpening sales and distribution capabilities.

Maggi noodles

Nestle's Maggi Noodles is a market leader in the Indian noodle market. Nestle has an 80 percent market share in the Rs 1,300 crore instant-noodle market and is credited with creating and nurturing the instant-noodle category in 1983.[4] In 2005, Maggi's brand value was Rs 370 crore vis-à-vis Rs 170 crore in 2003. Instant noodles comprise nearly 70 percent of India's noodle market. Maggi is a growth driver product for the company and accounts for 80 percent of the prepared-dishes category. A 30 percent growth rate over the last three years has fuelled 25 percent volume growth for the company.[5] Instant noodles have emerged as a viable snack-food option in India. It is expected that the category will continue to drive high double-digit growth in the coming years. Lack of serious competition so far has helped the product in maintaining a steep positive slope of its growth trajectory. Maggi Noodles is competing with Top Ramen, Sunfeast Pasta, Wai Wai, and a few private label brands such as Tasty Treat. Added to the growing competition driving up input costs, lower price increases and promotion of small packs is impacting its earnings before interest, taxes, depreciation and amortization (Ebitda) margins.

Maggi Noodles has become a favourite snack with children of all ages.[6] After 25 years it is now popular with many adults who have grown up eating Maggi Noodles during childhood. Advertising spending on Maggi Noodles has been the highest for noodle advertisement in the Indian market. Besides heavy budgets for advertisements, Nestle has been spending regularly on activities such as free samples in schools, in-shop promotions, and product display at points of sale. Reluanch after regular intervals of two–three years has been of immense benefit. Considering increased health concerns among consumers, the new punchline for the Maggi brand is 'Taste Bhi, Health Bhi'. The launch of a Rs 5 pack aided in penetrating deeper into existing markets. The brand has wide flavour options, from regular masala to chicken; or more localized flavours like curry, atta vegetable, lemon rice, and shahi pulao. Thus we see that the key factors which have contributed to Maggi's wide and deep penetration in the Indian market are: variety, ground-level promotions, affordable price point pack sizes (Rs 5 packs), heavy advertisement spending, regular relaunches, and high distribution capabilities. This demonstrates that in spite of being a market leader, strategic initiatives are needed on a regular basis for further growth and consolidation of the growth achieved.

Nirma

Nirma began operations as a one-product, one-man start-up in 1969 and has grown into a Rs 48 billion company within four decades.[7] The company currently has multiple manufacturing facilities and most of its products are under the Nirma brand umbrella. The company's mission to provide 'Better Products, Better Value, Better Living' has made a significant contribution to its success. Nirma countered competition from Hindustan Lever Ltd (HLL) and carved a niche for itself in the lower end of the detergent and toilet soap market. It later launched products for the upper end of the market to retain its middle-class consumers who could rise to the upper end.

Nirma's washing powder was extremely competitive. It was priced at Rs 3.50 per kg, at a time when HLL's Surf was priced at Rs 15. Gradually, Nirma started penetrating into HLL's market share. By 1985, Nirma washing powder had become one of the most popular detergent brands in many parts of the country. By 1999, Nirma was a major FMCG brand, offering a range of detergents, soaps, and personal care products.

Nirma's success in the highly competitive soaps and detergents market can be attributed to its product promotion efforts. These were mostly trade promotions, that is, huge margins passed on to retailers. For example, for Nirma premium soap, the company offered 52 percent and for Nirma shampoo, it offered an unbelievable margin of 140 percent to retailers. The company also focused on its distribution reach and market penetration to complement its promotion of efforts. Nirma's network consists of more than 400 distributors and over 2 million retail outlets across the country. This huge network enabled Nirma's products to penetrate into points of sale in the smallest village.[8] Nirma's ad spending was very low compared to other FMCG companies. While the normal advertising budgets were 6–10 percent of the companies' turnover, Nirma spent only 1.25–2 percent. Even celebrities used for soap endorsements were starlets like Sangeeta Bijlani, Sonali Bendre, and Riya Sen, who were relatively unknown at that time. The advertisement messages were also very simple and focused on the benefit of the product. Another factor which facilitated penetration of Nirma's products into the market was its focus on cost effectiveness.

Excessive focus on cost effectiveness caused Nirma to be considered as a cheap brand and many high-market people were not comfortable using this brand. To shed this lowly image, in the late 1990s Nirma released corporate advertisements worth Rs 10 billion throughout India. With increased rivalry from different players (such as HLL, P&G, Henkel SPIC, and many other local brands), changing customer attitudes, and rising disposable income, Nirma's scope for growth has decreased significantly. If Nirma is to grow sustainably, the company needs to decide whether the cost-focused model will continue to work, or if it needs to be altered or complemented with further advertising. Improved distribution structure in urban markets will also be a deciding factor.

Leisure Hotels Limited—Initiatives in adventure and ecotourism segments

Leisure Hotels Limited is a major player in Uttarakhand's hospitality sector. Its portfolio of resorts and luxury camps incorporates beautiful properties in the state's scenic tourist destinations offering leisure, adventure, and spiritual retreats.[9] It started with its first venture at Nainital—The Naini Retreat. Since September 1989, the company has had the opportunity to serve the largest number of tourists in Uttarakhand at several locations. It has properties at Nainital, Corbett National Park, Hardwar, Rishikesh, Ramgarh, Dehradun, Ranikhet, as well as a property in Goa. Facing stiff competition from its competitors and a desire for growth encouraged the organization to promote the places it was operating with new communications. The initiatives it took were to service certain niche segments in the same markets using existing resources. All it did was project its services with a new position—focusing on the adventure and ecotourism markets, as well as spiritual tourism. As a part of these initiatives, Leisure Hotels started the Chardham Camps, an eco-friendly luxury tent accommodation for those wishing to go to the four holy sites of Badrinath, Kedarnath, Yamunotri, and Gangotri. The Char Dham package has become extremely popular with non-resident Indians. Chardham Camps is the first of its kind in the Uttarakhand region. The company has elephant/jeep safaris, nature walks/treks/hikes, birdwatching, whitewater rafting, rock climbing, river crossing and more as part of its adventure tourism package. With all this to offer, young people are also buying these packages.[10]

CONCLUSION

The option of market penetration is the least risky and seems to be one of the first options growth chasers should consider, as it demands comparatively less resources than do the other options of product development, new market development, or diversification. To churn maximum profits, organizations need to pay attention to the feedback of existing customers, be vigilant of competitive activities, leverage existing tangible and intangible strengths, and work upon internal growth barriers. Even for growth in existing markets with existing products, organizations have to become innovative in thinking of possible growth avenues, followed by designing a strategy, and implementing it meticulously to achieve the growth objective.

NOTES

1. P. Kotler, Keller, Kelvin, Koshy, A., and Jha, M. (2006). *Marketing Management: A South Asian Perspective*, New Delhi: Dorling Kindersley, ch. 9.

2. Roger J. Best, (2009). *Market-Based Management: Strategies for Growing Customer Value and Profitability*, New Jersey: Pearson Prentice Hall, ch.11.

3. Kotler, *et al.*, ch. 8.

4. Retrieved from http://www.livemint.com/2009/12/28203439/Nestle-to-remain-market-leader.htm dated 24 August 2010.

5. Retrieved from www.nestle.co.in, dated 24 August 2010.

6. Retrieved from http://www.merinews.com/article/maggi-still-rules-indian-taste-buds/15812442.shtml, dated 24 August 2010.

7. Retrieved from http://www.moneycontrol.com/annual-report/nirma/directors-report/N, dated 24 August 2010.

8. Retrieved from http://www.icmrindia.org/free%20resources/casestudies/The%20Nirma.htm, dated 24 August 2010.

9. Retrieved from http://www.leisurehotels.co.in/aboutus.html, dated 24 August 2010.

10. Retrieved from http://www.india-reports.com/NL-Travel/07/Aug-3.aspx, dated 24 August 2010.

2

Growth through Geographical Expansion

INTRODUCTION

In Chapter 1 we discussed how an organization can grow in existing markets using existing products. In this chapter we discuss how to grow beyond existing markets, focusing on growth beyond national territories. Though the discussion stresses transnational expansion, most issues and concepts discussed are relevant for expansion beyond existing territories (state or region) for a diverse country like India.

For a company with global aspirations, foreign market growth strategies should be evaluated against domestic ones. Once a foreign market entry decision is made, the next step is to plan that entry. Foreign market entry strategies involve decisions about the target market (country), entry mode, and control system.[1] The chosen entry mode significantly impacts the success of entry and performance of international operations. The process requires awareness of alternative modes available for a particular product market combination and a cost–benefit analysis of the same. The diversity of uncertainties faced by firms in foreign markets necessitates the balancing of control and flexibility in market entry decisions. It is a decision where managers have to decide which trade-offs they are ready to make. The uncertainties faced by firms in foreign markets demand a balance of control and flexibility in its market entry decisions[2].

ENTRY MODE OPTIONS

There are a variety of market entry strategies available to organizations that are interested in expanding into foreign markets, which can be broadly categorized as exporting, licensing, joint venture or strategic alliances, and wholly owned subsidiary.

Export

Exporting is one of the most preferred methods of entering into a foreign market, as the risk and investment involved is low. Many geographical markets are not large enough to set up manufacturing operations in those foreign markets. Also, when the target country markets comprise of several small markets, it is more beneficial to adopt the export mode of entry. There are several strategic objectives which are met by adoption of the export option of entry.[3] Some of these are as follows: a) the organization gains economies of scale because of higher capacity utilization at a single location, b) the organization learns to compete in the new environment without much investment, and hence limited risk, and c) such a move may help the organization overcome growth constraints in the markets in its home country.

Indirect exporting
The option of export can be executed directly or indirectly. Indirect export involves intermediaries, like agents or export trading

houses, that have marketing and distribution capabilities in the target country.

Firms that do not have sufficient resources can adopt the option of exporting through a consortium. This is an option usually adopted by smaller organizations by forming export associations, where each member enjoys the strength of the associations while maintaining its independence and identity. Also, this gives the smaller organizations access to markets which would have remained beyond their reach due to resource constraints. Key features of export through such a process are:

▶ A target export region is identified
▶ Organizations with complementary capabilities and resources enter into an agreement of exporting jointly
▶ The consortium of members is registered and managed as a company with a board of directors and its own employees

Products such as handicrafts and commodity products such as rubber, rice, dry fruit, mangoes, etc. are exported through such consortiums.

The option of indirect exporting can also be executed by exporting through brokers. Brokers are usually experts in handling exports to a specific region or country, or specific product groups. So, the organization can select the broker according to their expertise and take due diligence on who will be the most appropriate broker to meet the objectives of the organization. Brokers should be used by organizations that are infrequent exporters.

Advantages associated with indirect exporting are:

▶ The organization is able to focus on its core competencies
▶ It needs low resource commitments and is a low-risk option

- ▶ It provides a good learning experience for adoption of other options which require higher resource commitments and involve greater risks

Disadvantages of indirect exporting are as follows:

- ▶ Inadequate attention on services delivered, leading to long-term negative impact on the image of the organization
- ▶ Possibility of opportunity loss due to insufficient effort of the agents
- ▶ Lack of development of first-hand knowledge of the export market which could have been gained through owned operations

Direct exporting

When an organization directly deal with the customer in the foreign market it is considered as direct exporting. For direct exporting, organizations usually set up a company-owned sales office (foreign sales subsidiary) or intermediaries to manage sales and after-sales service. Organizations which target long-term growth from a concerned foreign market usually set up a sales office.

As revenue from the foreign market begins to rise, organizations commit more resources and take on higher risks. The next phase involves whether or not to continue serving these markets through exports or to grow through initiation of local manufacturing.

Licensing

Licensing is a process of charging a fee and/or royalty for allowing a patented technology, trademark, or brand name to be used by another organization for a specific period of time. This is one method of entering into a foreign market while committing limited resources. The resources committed and the risk involved in this mode are higher than serving foreign markets through exports, but less than those required for joint ventures, strategic alliances, or wholly owned subsidiaries. Licensing terms and period vary widely across organizations. Licensing is beneficial for an organization with limited resources for entering into foreign markets without making investments for plant and machinery or infrastructure for distribution. The pitfalls of such a mode of foreign market entry are that it results in limited returns for the licenser, and the licensee may not give due attention to long-term market development.

Other options for foreign market entry which involve relatively low commitments of resources and are similar to licensing are *franchising, contract manufacturing, turnkey projects, and management contracts.*

In a franchising agreement, the franchiser transfers the right to use its brand name, process know-how, or copyright to the franchisee. This is usually more prevalent in service industries such as fast food, retailing, education, and hotels. McDonald's and Domino's Pizza scaled up their international business using this mode for expansion. This allows the franchising organization access to local entrepreneurs, their knowledge of local customers and legal bodies. The franchising organization should also be careful that product and service quality standards adhere to the norms stated.

Contract manufacturing is preferred in situations when the product technology is widely known and the success of an organization in a foreign market is dependent on the marketing capabilities of the organization. Such agreements usually are for a long term.

In a turnkey agreement, the contractor takes complete responsibility for a project, from conceptualization to installation and training of users. After commissioning, the contractor will have to operate the plant for a specified duration before handing it over to the client. The pricing of such a product is fixed price or cost plus pricing. While in the former the contractor bears the risk, in the case of the later, the risk is with the client. This mode of entry is more common in industries such as petrochemicals, chemicals, power generation, etc.

Management contracts as a mode of entry are used widely in the field of services, such as hotels or privately managed hospitals. This process involves transfer of management know-how and technology from one organization to another. This mode of entry is preferred when scarcity of resources in target markets (availability of managerial expertise) or legal hurdles disallow owned manufacturing in a foreign country.

Joint Ventures and Strategic Alliances

A joint venture is the creation of a separate firm whose equity is shared by two or more partners, each expecting dividends proportional to their shareholdings.[4] Strategic alliances are an arrangement between organizations wherein these organizations come together to fulfill a specific core business objective. The alliance may be registered as a separate legal entity, or may be just a make-shift arrangement. The alliance, as an entity, passes through different stages of its life cycle; each stage is unique in nature, and so are the factors that decide whether the alliance will be able to address the challenges of that stage and pass to the next stage or not. Three major stages (the beginning of partner selection and alliance formation, formation of norms and structure of the alliance, and management of the alliance) that a strategic alliance undergoes have different critical success factors. How growth can be pursued by using joint ventures and strategic alliances as a mode of entry in foreign markets and what issues are to be taken care of, will be discussed in depth in Chapter 7. Partners in joint ventures and strategic alliances bring in complementary resources and capabilities. These require much larger resource commitments vis-à-vis any of the entry modes discussed earlier. Seeds of discontent may develop if any of the assumptions presupposed by any of the partners during the due diligence phase go wrong, or discontent may develop as a result of certain actions by a partner.

Wholly owned subsidiary

An organization aspiring to be firmly present in foreign markets can do so through a wholly owned subsidiary. This mode involves the highest commitment of resources, and hence involves the highest risks as well as returns. An organization may start operations by acquisition of an existing organization, or any of its resources (factory or brand), or through greenfield investments. Wholly owned subsidiaries give complete control to the organization and thus a potential conflict which may arise in a joint venture or strategic alliance is avoided. Also, the potential gap in efforts which may arise in the case of exporting and licensing is avoided when an organization decides to opt for the wholly owned subsidiary mode of entry.

FACTORS INFLUENCING ENTRY MODE CHOICE

The choice of entry mode is focused on factors such as market potential, country risk, location familiarity, competitive scenario, transaction-specific factors, as well as strategic and organizational factors. Broadly, the factors can be categorized as internal factors, target country factors, and home country factors.[5]

Internal factors

Internal factors influencing the choice of entry mode are firm size, product type, available resources, global strategy, international experience, and management perception.

Firm size: Size (turnover, number of employees, number of countries in which it has a presence, product variety, etc.) is a critical factor in the choice of entry mode. The size of the firm has influence on several other factors directly or indirectly and is therefore one of the most important factors influencing the choice of entry mode. Larger firms would have a larger variety of differentiated products, existing for a longer period of time; would have excess resources to commit, capacity to absorb risks, higher need for growth, and capacity to fuel this growth. The entry mode alternatives available to a larger firm are much more than are available to a smaller firm, thus it has the ability to take higher risks.

An organization's product portfolio: This broadly refers to the capability of the company to develop different products or its existing portfolio of differentiated products. Product-related factors such as the type of product (differentiated products, standard products, service-intensive products, service products, technology-intensive products, low product adaptation, and high product adaptation) also influence the choice of entry mode.[6] Highly differentiated products with distinct advantages over competitive products give sellers the advantage of commanding a higher price and hence they can absorb additional costs of exporting and still maintain a significantly good margin.

An alternative view is when a firm possesses the capability to develop differentiated products, it may risk loss of long-term revenues if it shares this knowledge with host country firms. In such cases, the higher control modes may be preferred. Thus, decision makers need to judge their organization's product design capabilities to decide which mode of entry to opt for.

Availability of resources: The availability of resources (limited or substantial resources) and the level of commitment towards targeted foreign operations also may influence the entry decision. The more abundant the resources of the company related to management, capital, technology, production skills, and marketing, the more numerous its entry mode options. Limited resources constrain the option to modes which require less resource commitment.

Globalization strategy and internationalization experience of the firm: The degree of commitment is also determined by the importance accorded to internationalization in a firm's corporate strategy. When the firm believes that a significant strategic control in a foreign market can help it realize global synergies then it may choose a mode of entry that gives higher control.[7] This is also influenced by any of the firm's earlier successes or failures in international ventures. The degree to which it has succeeded or failed using a particular entry mode would decide what entry mode it would prefer in its future foreign ventures.

Management attitude and perception: Managerial perceptions are also relevant for the assessment of the location advantages of a specific country.[8] Managerial perceptions may be different due to variations in managers' past experiences in that country (and other countries), levels of knowledge about that country and individual biases.

Target country external factors

While evaluating the external factors in selection of entry mode strategy, both the *target country's external factors* and the *home country's external factors* should be examined.

The target country's external factors that influence the choice of entry mode are market size, production factors, macro- and microeconomic factors, social factors, government regulation, available market infrastructure, location advantage, cultural distance between home country and host country. Of these factors, those that are critically important are discussed below.

Target country market factors: The present or projected size of the target market is an important factor to be considered while deciding the mode of entry. Small market size favours entry modes that have a low break-even sales volume (indirect exporting or contractual arrangements). Conversely, markets with high sales potential can justify an entry mode which requires higher resource commitments and are more risky.

Target country production factors: The quality, quantity, and cost of raw materials, labour, energy and other production factors; as well as cost and quality of available economic infrastructure (transportation, communication, port facilities, etc.) also influence the choice of entry mode.

Target country environmental factors: The political, economic, and socio-cultural character of the target country can have decisive influence on the entry mode. Perhaps most influential are government policies and regulations relating to operations of foreign firms and international business. Within policies and regulations, import policies and foreign investment policies are more critical. The micro- and macro-economic factors of the target country's economy, such as its size (measured by GDP), per capita income, and the relative importance of economic sectors (as percentage of GDP) must also be considered before a choice of entry mode is made. Favourable dynamic factors may justify entry modes with high break-even points, even when the current market size is below the break-even point. This is due to expectation of high market growth in the long term.

Cultural distance between home and host country: As the cultural distance between the home and host countries increases, committing more resources for entry into a new market becomes riskier. Cultural distance can have opposite effects on the choice of entry modes. In situations of high cultural distance, wherein the MNC lacks sufficient knowledge to operate on its own, it may rely on a local partner to contribute local knowledge and thus would prefer a low-control entry mode, such as licensing or contractual modes. On the other hand, it may opt for a high-control mode (that is, wholly owned subsidiary) as a way of reducing dependence on local agents whose behaviour may be difficult to understand.

Home country external factors

Important home country factors are related to market, production, and environment. Firms operating in larger home country markets tend to use equity modes of entry. Also, firms that operate in more competitive environments prefer a direct investment mode of entry. Other home country factors which influence foreign entry decision are: a) production costs in the home country relative to costs in target foreign country, and b) policy of the home government related to export and foreign investment by domestic firms. If the government offers tax holidays and similar incentives for exporting, but at the same time is neutral or restrictive towards foreign direct investment, the firms may favour contractual modes of entry. The home country government may have strict regulations related to pollution or higher costs for carbon emissions; this may lead the firms to invest in manufacturing facilities overseas.

Born globals

The view that an organization evaluates the option of international growth only when the internal market potential is exhausted—or when the organization has gained sufficient experience in its home country—is no longer sacrosanct. With advances in technology and communication, some organizations are venturing into international transactions from infancy. These organizations are termed 'Born Globals'. This new phenomenon may be attributed to increasing globalization, relaxation in restrictive regulations, new developments in transportation and communication technologies, and the growing number of people with international experience. A distinguishing feature of 'born global' organizations is an international focus very early in their journey (at times right from inception), and the same being demonstrated by observable and significant commitments of resources (for example, material, people, financing, time) in more than one nation. Thus, smaller or newly born organizations need not always wait to gain a firm foothold in a home country before evaluating growth options in international markets.

ILLUSTRATIONS

Illustration 1: Kellogg's entry into the Indian market

Kellogg started their operations in the United States in 1894, and by 1995, it was a multinational company with operations in eighteen countries, with products available in 160 countries, and a turnover of USD7 billion.[9] By this time, the US breakfast cereal market had matured, and year-on-year growth rates were not moving beyond single digits, and were being considered as saturated. Lured by the prospect of a billion breakfast eaters, India was identified as one of the potential markets of future growth. The changing, post-liberalization business environment in India made it more business friendly. Kellogg wanted to do things slowly. India was first considered as a vital future market in 1986, and a liaison office was set up in Delhi. Options such as forming a joint venture were evaluated but rejected. For Kellogg, control of operations was more critical and therefore they were in favour of an option that would provide them more control of Indian operations. They were looking for at least 51 percent control. So, they waited until such an opportunity arose. In 1992, they gained permission to set up a 51 percent owned subsidiary.[10] They planned to offer the balance stake to the public. That idea was later dropped, and in 1994 they got permission to set up a 100 percent wholly owned subsidiary. But, having decided to go for it alone, Kellogg had to build things from scratch. Before this, the entry of most consumer product MNCs into the Indian market—such as that of Procter & Gamble and Duracell—had been through joint ventures to leverage the distribution capabilities of the Indian partner. There were several teething problems that Kellogg faced in the initial years. Later, Kellogg did almost everything that any best books on international marketing would suggest to build brand Kellogg in India, but they possibly could not understand Indian food habits and the psychology of Indian homemakers. It is difficult to identify what specifically went wrong, but possibly, an Indian partner could have helped Kellogg understand consumers better than what they did by themselves[11]. Moving in as a subsidiary, expecting to repeat the western world success story in India, overlooking the cultural roots and habits associated with traditional breakfast in India, was possibly not the best strategy.

Illustration 2: Nike, Inc.'s entry into India through Licensing

Nike, a major global player in sports, fitness, shoes, and other accessories decided to enter into India in the mid-1990s through an exclusive licensing arrangement with Siera Industrial Enterprise Private Limited (SIEPL). Nike was to receive royalties, which was a certain percent of its net sales revenue. Nike's marketing objective was to tap the Indian sports-and-fitness shoe market—7 million pairs of shoes. Nike positioned itself in the premium niche segment. Rather than cricket, the focus was on basketball and tennis. The performance of Nike in India was not far below expectations. This allowed the company to change its plan from 100 percent imports to localization of the product. This also made the product more affordable. Distribution company-owned and franchise-operated showrooms opened. Earlier, Bata showrooms were the only channels of distribution. During this period, sales were underperforming and Nike's exposure was minimal, as it was operating though a licensee. Later in the year 2004, once[12] the company had achieved sufficient stronghold in the Indian market and had some insights on how to operate in India, it did not renew the agreement with Siera and became a subsidiary.[13] Critics believe that because of choosing licensing as a mode of entry Nike took much more time to adapt to the needs of Indian consumers vis-à-vis its competitor Reebok.

Illustration 3: Bridgestone 's—entry into India through a Joint venture with ACC Ltd

Bridgestone, the largest rubber and tyre company in the world, incorporated in Japan in 1931, entered India in 1996. The organization chose to set up a joint venture with ACC Limited. Bridgestone had 64 percent holdings in the joint venture, which focused solely on radial tyres for passenger cars. The joint venture was able to get OEM status for all Hundyai and Matiz cars in its first year of operations. Getting the same status from other car manufacturers was part of the future growth plan.[14] The experience and contacts of Bridgestone helped the joint venture in getting new contracts. Currently, Bridgestone enjoys OEM status for most of the major automobile manufactures operating in India. Usual policy for Bridgestone's international market entry was a 100 percent wholly owned subsidiary. But the Indian market was culturally different from others, it already knew. So Bridgestone decided to enter India as a joint venture to benefit from partners' knowledge of the Indian market. Later it transformed into a wholly owned subsidiary.

CONCLUSION

Thus, we observe that at one extreme, an organization can internationalize operations and perform all functions itself by establishing a subsidiary. At the other extreme, it may opt not to perform any of these functions in a foreign market, but to export through third-party distributors, saving on asset costs in the host country and thus reducing risks. A firm may also opt to use intermediate options such as licensed manufacturing, international joint ventures or strategic alliances. Generally, a firm's entry mode choices are determined by resource availability and the need for control.[15] Resource availability refers to the financial and managerial capacity of a firm for serving a particular foreign market. Control refers to a firm's need to influence systems, methods, and decisions in a foreign market.[16] Control is desirable to improve a firm's competitive position and maximize the returns on its assets and skills. Higher operational control results from having a greater ownership in the foreign venture. However, risks are also likely to be higher due to the assumption of responsibility for decision-making and a higher commitment of resources. Entry mode choices are often a compromise between these attributes. The exporting mode is a low resource commitment (investment) and consequently, a low risk–return alternative. This mode, while providing the firm with operational control, lacks in providing marketing control that may be essential for market-seeking firms. The owned venture, on the other hand, is a big investment and consequently, a high risk–return alternative that also provides a high degree of control to the investing firm. The joint venture requires relatively lower investment and hence involves risk, return, and control proportionate to the extent of equity participation of the investing firm. Finally, the licensing option is a low investment (low compared to owned ventures or joint ventures), low risk–return alternative which provides lower control (low compared to owned ventures or joint ventures but higher than export option) to the licensing firm.[17]

NOTES

1. Root, F.R. (1977). *Entry Strategies for Foreign Markets: From Domestic to International Business*. New York: Amacom.

2. Root, F.R. (1994). *Entry Strategies for International Markets*. New York: Lexington Books.

3. Chaudhuri, S. and Das, R. (2001). *Entry Strategies and Growth in Foreign Markets: Text and Cases in the Indian Context*. New Delhi: Oxford University Press.

4. Contractor F.J. and Lorange, P. (1988). *Cooperative Strategies in International Business*. Lexington: Lexington Books.

5. The discussion in this section has drawn heavily from a working paper of Sabyasachi Sinha (2009) (doctoral student, IIM Ahmedabad), titled 'Factors that Influence Foreign Market Entry Mode Strategy'.

6. Chaudhuri and Das (2001).

7. Taylor, C.R., Zou, S., and Osland, G.E. (2000). 'Foreign Market Entry Strategy of Japanese MNCs, *International Journal of Marketing Review*, 17 (2), pp. 146–63.

8. Miles, R.E., Snow, C.C., and Meyer, A.D. (1978). *Organization Strategy, Structure and Process*. New York: McGraw Hill.

9. Chaudhuri and Das (2001), pp. 79–92.

10. Chaudhuri and Das (2001).

11. Retrieved from http://www.ftpress.com/articles/article.aspx?p=101588&seqNum=3, dated 30 August 2010. Retrieved from http://communications.webalne.com/2009/09/14/branding-mishaps-kellogs-india-menture-a-jailure/28 August 2010.

12. Chaudhuri and Das (2001), pp. 223–4.

13. Retrieved from http://www.rediff.com/money/2006/nov/14spec1.htm on 28 August 2010.

14. Retrieved from http://www.financialexpress.com/news/bridgestonehashelpedinfrasterradialisationofindianmarket/74724/0 on 28 August 2010.

FIGURE 3.1

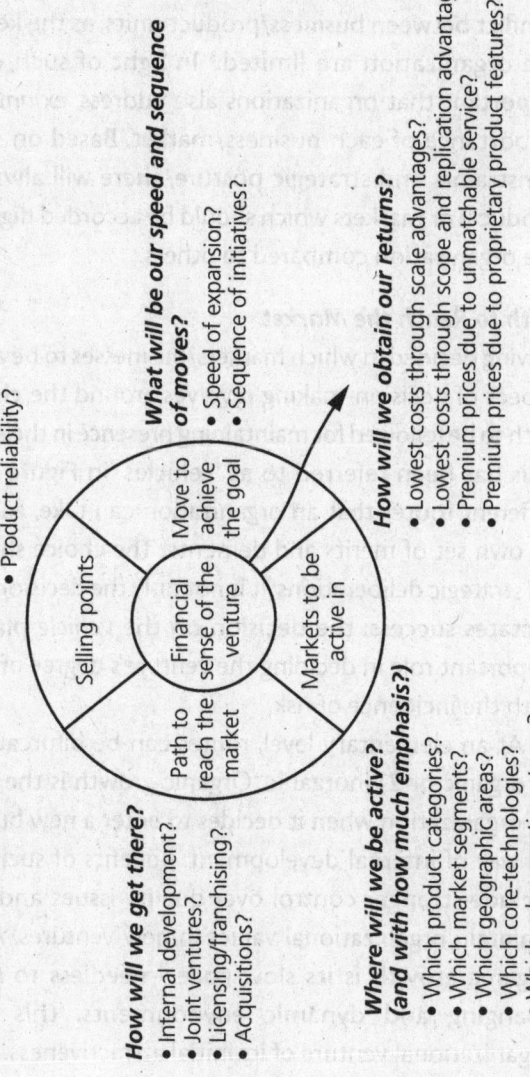

How will we win?
- Image?
- Customization?
- Price?
- Styling?
- Product reliability?

What will be our speed and sequence of moves?
- Speed of expansion?
- Sequence of initiatives?

How will we obtain our returns?
- Lowest costs through scale advantages?
- Lowest costs through scope and replication advantages?
- Premium prices due to unmatchable service?
- Premium prices due to proprietary product features?

Where will we be active? (and with how much emphasis?)
- Which product categories?
- Which market segments?
- Which geographic areas?
- Which core-technologies?
- Which value-creation stages?

How will we get there?
- Internal development?
- Joint ventures?
- Licensing/franchising?
- Acquisitions?

Selling points

Financial sense of the venture

Move to achieve the goal

Path to reach the market

Markets to be active in

SOURCE: HAMBRICK AND FREDRICKSON, 2001

There are organizations that are (or intend to be) active in multiple businesses/markets. Such situations often lead to internal conflict between business/product units, as the key resources of the organization are limited.[3] In light of such conflicts, it is important that organizations also address, *ex ante*, the relative importance of each business/market. Based on such resource constraints and strategic posture, there will always be certain products or markets which should be accorded higher priority by the organization compared to others.

Path to Reach the Market

Having decided in which markets/businesses to be active, the next aspect of decision-making revolves around the challenge of the path to be followed for maintaining presence in the said businesses. This has been referred to as 'vehicles' in Figure 3.1. There are different routes that an organization can take, each one having its own set of merits and demerits. The choice should be based on strategic deliberations. It is not only the decision on *arena* that dictates success; the decision on the *vehicle* plays an equally important role in deciding the venture's degree of success, along with the incidence of risk.

At an elementary level, routes can be bifurcated into either 1) organic or 2) inorganic. Organic growth is the path taken by an organization when it decides to enter a new business/market by way of internal development. Benefits of such a movement include stronger control over quality issues and the ability to maintain organizational values in new ventures. A key pitfall of organic growth is its slow pace—needless to say, in rapidly changing and dynamic environments, this can rob the organizational venture of its initial attractiveness.

Inorganic growth is the route taken by an organization when it decides to grow by either collaborating/merging with or

15. Stopford, J.M. and Wells, L.T. (1972). *Managing the Multinational Enterprise*. New York: Basic Books.
16. Anderson, E. and Gatignon, H. (1986). 'Modes of Foreign Entry: A Transaction Cost Analysis and Propositions,' *Journal of International Business Studies*, 17(3), pp. 1–26.
17. Chaudhuri and Das (2001), pp. 224–5.

3

Growth through New Product or New Market Scope

INTRODUCTION

This chapter is dedicated to an understanding of how organizations grow by expanding their market presence through their products/services. Such multidimensional decisions are complex, and should be made based on intense deliberation, taking into account the nuances the new product/service will face in the market. The chapter begins by throwing some light on alternative growth trajectories, followed by a detailed section explaining the process of decision-making as it relates to the direction of growth. Subsequent to this, we elaborate on other factors that decide the direction of growth, such as industry attractiveness (an external factor) and the development of alternative growth avenues (an internal factor). We end with the examples of the Tata Nano and Bharat Forge, to show how multidimensional decision making is put into practice to channel growth for a new product in a new market.

ALTERNATIVE GROWTH TRAJECTORIES

The decision to grow is not enough for an organization to do so successfully. The organization needs to decide in which direction it wants to grow. Below are available alternatives, taking into account different combinations of products/services and markets.

The first alternative is, of course, for an organization to continue to sell the same product line to the existing market. Growth would then be accomplished by the efforts to increase sales. Known as *market penetration*[1], this may be achieved by selling more to the current customer base, or by wooing other customers in the same market. A detailed analysis of this alternative is already covered in Chapter 1.

A second alternative is to develop altogether new markets for the same product/serivce. Since each market's unique attributes are a result of a host of dynamics, such a move may require the organization to alter a few product attributes to suit the market. This endeavour of *market development* is detailed in Chapter 2.

A third way is to develop a new product in the same target market: *product development*. This is generally a preferred route of growth, given the organization's familiarity of movements in the market. This strategy requires good innovation capabilities, as covered in Chapter 5.

Last but not the least, an organization may grow by simultaneous movement into new product and market domains. This strategy of *diversification* is covered in Chapter 6. This strategy is very resource intensive, and may actually be a result of some micro-staged movements; this is explained in the sub-section 'Moves to Achieve the Goal' of this chapter.

Decision on the Direction to Grow

Once an organization has decided to grow, other decisions immediately follow. These decisions revolve around concerns such as intended markets and how to be successful in them, the basis on which the organization will ensure that it is perceived differently from the competition by targeted consumers, the sequence required to reach the target, and finally, the basis of ensuring that the entire business pursuit leads to profit.[2] Often, organizations tend to focus on only a small aspect of these necessary decisions. But detailed deliberation on the issues mentioned above will ensure robust decision-making about the proposed growth. This section is dedicated to an understanding of all these aspects.

Markets to be Active In

This aspect addresses which businesses the organization intends to be (or in which it already is) active. This has been referred to as 'arenas' in Figure 3.1. Prima facie, it seems that this is a single decision. However, it is essentially a set of other sub-questions, and answering these sub-questions leads an organization to decide the *arena* in which it intends to be active. These decisions range from 1) whether to grow by coming up with new products/services, 2) targeting existing products to a new segment of prospective customers, 3) entering new geographical territories, to 4) developing expertise in delivering the value proposition to customers. While making these decisions, the organization needs to ensure that it is as specific as possible, since there is always a tendency to make visionary statements which are difficult to follow through. As an example, 'To become the world's leading Consumer Company for automotive products and services' is a vision statement for Ford, but it does not qualify in the criteria set that we have enumerated as *arena* for an organization.

There are organizations that are (or intend to be) active in multiple businesses/markets. Such situations often lead to internal conflict between business/product units, as the key resources of the organization are limited.[3] In light of such conflicts, it is important that organizations also address, *ex ante*, the relative importance of each business/market. Based on such resource constraints and strategic posture, there will always be certain products or markets which should be accorded higher priority by the organization compared to others.

Path to Reach the Market

Having decided in which markets/businesses to be active, the next aspect of decision-making revolves around the challenge of the path to be followed for maintaining presence in the said businesses. This has been referred to as 'vehicles' in Figure 3.1. There are different routes that an organization can take, each one having its own set of merits and demerits. The choice should be based on strategic deliberations. It is not only the decision on *arena* that dictates success; the decision on the *vehicle* plays an equally important role in deciding the venture's degree of success, along with the incidence of risk.

At an elementary level, routes can be bifurcated into either 1) organic or 2) inorganic. Organic growth is the path taken by an organization when it decides to enter a new business/market by way of internal development. Benefits of such a movement include stronger control over quality issues and the ability to maintain organizational values in new ventures. A key pitfall of organic growth is its slow pace—needless to say, in rapidly changing and dynamic environments, this can rob the organizational venture of its initial attractiveness.

Inorganic growth is the route taken by an organization when it decides to grow by either collaborating/merging with or

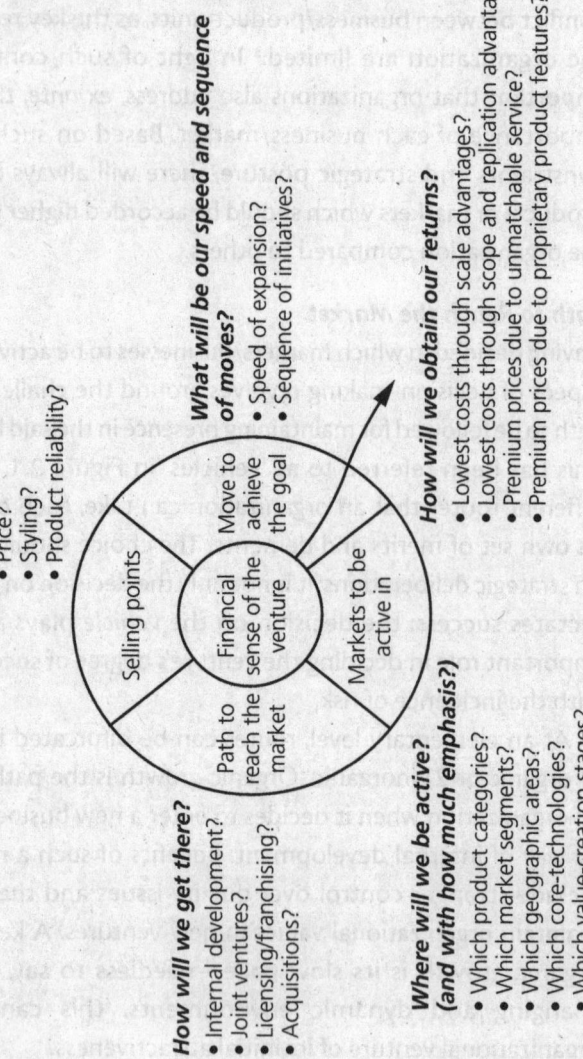

FIGURE 3.1

How will we win?
- Image?
- Customization?
- Price?
- Styling?
- Product reliability?

What will be our speed and sequence of moves?
- Speed of expansion?
- Sequence of initiatives?

How will we obtain our returns?
- Lowest costs through scale advantages?
- Lowest costs through scope and replication advantages?
- Premium prices due to unmatchable service?
- Premium prices due to proprietary product features?

Selling points

Move to achieve the goal

Financial sense of the venture

Path to reach the market

Markets to be active in

How will we get there?
- Internal development?
- Joint ventures?
- Licensing/franchising?
- Acquisitions?

Where will we be active? (and with how much emphasis?)
- Which product categories?
- Which market segments?
- Which geographic areas?
- Which core-technologies?
- Which value-creation stages?

SOURCE: HAMBRICK AND FREDRICKSON, 2001

acquiring other organizations. Collaboration can take various forms, such as licensing of the value proposition, franchising, or even joint ventures (both equity and non-equity forms are equally prevalent nowadays). The beauty of inorganic growth is the speed with which the organization can move into the new market. Such growth also helps bring in new partners, who can bring key resources necessary for growth which were otherwise unavailable (or scarce). However, there is a catch—the organization needs to be extra careful with inorganic growth, as it is difficult to maintain quality levels in the venture with new partners coming in. Also, the organization needs to take cognizance of the fact that collaboration requires idiosyncratic capabilities, which the organization requires to succeed.

Selling Points

The competitive landscape of today's environment dictates that the value proposition the organization offers should be perceived by customers to be different from that of competitors. Thus, there needs to be some 'differentiators' of the venture. Differentiators can take various forms, the popular among them being 1) lower price, 2) better product features for the same price as the competition, 3) custom-made features to cater to individual needs, 4) the image that the brand carries, and 5) greater dependability. These selling points are based on the entire value proposition offered by the organization, and need not be focused on individually. Ideally, an organization should possess a combination of the features above, in such a way that the competition finds it difficult to counter or even imitate. Like the previous aspect, we have a catch here as well—the choice of selling points should be such that they are coherent with each other. In a pursuit to achieve each one, organizations should not attempt to pump all the differentiators into a single product/service.

There is another decision that needs to be taken while choosing selling points. The organization needs to decide, *ex ante*, how the value proposition, along with its features, is to be sold as being different from the competition. At the same time, the organization needs to understand that the relative importance of a particular feature may need to change over time in order to sustain differentiation. This takes into account certain unpredictable moves from the competition. Now, tweaking the selling points is a delicate art, and should be a result of due deliberation. Any incompatibility in the differentiators arising out of such an alteration can be disastrous.

Moves to Achieve the Goal

The actual series of steps that an organization needs to take to move into the chosen *arena* is an important aspect of the decision to grow. After all, it is not only the end goal, but also the means to achieve the goal, that dictates the degree of the venture's success. This has been referred to as 'staging' in Figure 3.1, and has two aspects: 1) the speed at which the moves are made, and 2) the moves' sequence.

Speed is important to ensure that the competition is not able to catch up, but the speed needs to be controlled and pre-decided. This is because there are learning curve effects. An organization needs to have the ability to not only learn from each step, but also to integrate this learning back into the organizational routines to ensure that this learning can be utilized for further ventures and growth. If movement into the arena is done too quickly, then integrating the learning back into the venture will not be possible. At the same time, if the organization moves slowly to ensure deep integration of the learning back into the venture, then there are chances that the competition will overtake them. Hence, there is always a trade-off associated with the chosen speed of entering such a venture. As discussed earlier, if higher speed is sought, then the organization should aspire to grow inorganically. Similarly, if slower speed but greater learning and control are the keys to success, organic growth is better.

Sequencing moves is also very important. After all, it is not advisable for an organization to be present simultaneously in new geographies with multiple new value propositions at once. To understand this better, take a situation where an organization has decided to come up with a broad array of products to be marketed in a range of territories. This involves two uncertainties—one relates to product features, the other to the dynamics of a new market. It is better if the organization decides to tackle one uncertainty at a time. It may decide to first strengthen its product base by launching products in an existing market. Once successful in the current market with its range of products, the organization may decide to enter new markets with the pre-tested products. Alternatively, it may first enter new markets with a narrow range of products already available. Once successful in this range of markets with current products, the organization may decide to launch a new range in pre-tested markets.

Financial Sense of the Venture

An organizational pursuit to grow should be ultimately motivated by the ability of the new venture to add to the organization's net profit. Figure 3.1 depicts this as 'financial sense of the venture'. Sources of such financial sensibility could be multiple, ranging from an increase in net profit to cost reduction. Ultimately, the venture should add to the profit margin. Some ventures may be such that they lead to outright increase in profit because of the value proposition's premium positioning. However, there can be other, more subtle, financial advantages. For example, some ventures on a stand-alone basis might seem unprofitable. However, when viewed with existing businesses of the organization, they may seem lucrative because of cost advantages arising out of scale or scope economies. An economy of scale is the cost advantage that an organization derives by increasing the production or sale of a product, because by such increase in scale, the average cost per unit falls. On similar lines, an economy of scope is the cost advantage that an organization derives by using existing facilities to produce or distribute other products/services.

An organization, while deriving the economic sense of a venture, should not be purely driven by the absolute magnitude of expected profit. After all, funds are being invested. As a result, the venture should generate profits that are higher than the cost of capital that has been invested. Needless to say, there is no financial sense in a venture which generates profits which can alternatively be earned by simply investing the funds in extant bonds.

ADDITIONAL ATTRIBUTES AFFECTING THE DIRECTION OF GROWTH

Industry Attractiveness

The degree of an industry's attractiveness is an important criterion while deciding on the direction to grow. Before embarking on the journey of understanding the attributes of industry attractiveness, it is important for us to understand what industry means. There are two parameters that define an industry—one is products or services, the other is geography. There are five forces that help us understand the attractiveness of an industry[4]: the threat of new entrants, the threat of substitutes, the bargaining power of suppliers, the bargaining power of buyers, and rivalry amongst existing competitors. These five forces, better known as the Porter's

5-Forces framework. If the combination of these five forces is low, then the industry is attractive and profitable. Prior to entering an industry, an organization must carry out an analysis of its attractiveness.

Entry into an attractive industry is definitely a recipe for growth. However, such growth is contingent upon the growth of the industry as a whole. Once the industry reaches maturity and growth plateaus, the growth of organizations in the industry is also affected. Under such circumstances, growth means the acquisition of other players, though it has been proven that such acquisitions often lead to destruction of shareholder wealth. The next section discusses an alternative growth tool for organizations not operating in very attractive industries.

Alternative Growth Avenues

We discuss here the alternative growth avenues that enable an organization to grow by extension of its capabilities into new (and not previously explored) domains. These growth avenues also been referred to as new growth platforms.[5] They can be used to address latent or unmet customer demand. To deliver the value proposition to customers, the organization may have to modify its capabilities. Alteration of capability-sets is often a tedious task, as in-house alterations may not always be possible. In such cases, it is important that such capabilities are sourced from other organizations, in the form of collaborations, or even acquisitions.

The creation of alternative growth avenues often requires the team to think out of the box. This is possible if—and only if—such a team is shielded from the organization's day-to-day operations, given financial leeway, and autonomy and independence in decision-making. The process of forming such driving departments should also be institutionalized, as this will ensure that participation in the unit is based purely on merit and not politics.

ILLUSTRATIONS

Illustration I: The Tata Nano

The chairman of Tata Motors, part of the Tata Group, had dreamt of marketing an affordable car for India's middle-income group for Rs 1 lakh. But their creative approach was to target not existing or potential car owners but those who were driving two-wheelers. A good quality two-wheeler was priced at around Rs 60,000. Therefore, if a company could make and offer an automobile for around Rs 1,00,000[6], it could migrate a large section of two-wheeler drivers into four-wheeler driver segment, thereby creating an altogether new customer base—somewhere between an average two-wheeler and a Maruti 800 car.

In 2003[7], a four-member team at Tata Motors was shown a very fluid brief of an advance engineering project. The idea was to try and create a very low-cost vehicle with four wheels—it was not even defined as a car.

What was defined was the cost: Rs 1 lakh without compromising on aesthetics, value to the customer, or safety and environment requirements (at the time, the smallest car in India cost around Rs 2.5 lakh). Chairman Ratan Tata was very clear that it had to be a complete car.

The Tata Nano was finally launched in March 2009, without compromising on the targeted price tag of Rs 1 lakh. Tata Motors plans to export the car to newer territories, such as emerging economies in Asia, Latin America and Africa. Targeting these countries is intuitive, given that they share similar regulatory dynamics and market maturity. Thus, we see that first a new product is developed and launched in a known territory, followed by attempts to expand in newer markets. Hence, a decision on the *arena* is not sufficient; the *staging* has an equal role in deciding the degree of an endeavour's success.

Illustration II: Bharat Forge Limited

Bharat Forge Limited (BFL) is one of the most innovative and exciting organizations to emerge in the history of the forging industry. It came into existence in 1961 (and commenced operations in 1966[8]) to meet the forging needs of the Indian automotive industry during a time of nominal ancillaries, scarce infrastructure, and import-ruled industries.

The 1970s witnessed a spurt in the Indian forging industry, and for BFL, it was a period of consolidation and growth. With the largest integrated facilities in Asia and an unbeatable track record, BFL emerged as the undisputed leader of the forging industry in India.

With an emphasis on diversification, the 1980s saw BFL grow from a primarily automotive ancillary to an engineering enterprise focusing on technological supremacy, resilience, and total customer orientation. An outstanding reputation for customer service coupled with the management's commitment to quality has made BFL the preferred domestic and global supplier for major OEMs across the global forging automotive industry.

Over a period of time, BFL ensured it was present in not only multiple products but also multiple markets[9]. The product range of the organization encompasses crankshafts, axle beams, transmission parts—catering to small to heavy vehicles—rods, shafts, and casing—catering to a vast array of industries ranging from sugar to energy. BFL did not become present in these industries overnight, nor was it a single-stage movement. Having decided to be present in industries (that is, arena) such as sugar, energy, shipping, petroleum, automobiles, etc., the next stage was to decide the series of steps to be taken to be successfully integrated in those industries (that is, staging). If we observe closely, alternative growth avenues were chosen very carefully to ensure that there wasn't any paradigm shift in the capability set of the organization. All BFL products were manufactured using die forging; the big difference was the way the die forging was done. For example, products targeting the transport industry are a result of closed die forging, and products targeting other industries are a result of open die forging. BFL has nine manufacturing facilities spread across six countries. As per the current estimate, it is the world's second largest forging company.

CONCLUSION

Of the four elementary alternatives available to expand an organization (Alternative Growth Trajectories), the decision to grow both with new products and in new markets is the most challenging one. To reap benefits from this decision, it is important that organizations follow a structured process to both 1) arrive at the decision, and 2) to execute the decision. The five aspects of such a process are expected to give a clear-cut picture of not only the way in which the decision to grow will be implemented, but also of the nature of benefits that the organization will derive from the decision ('Decision on Direction to Grow'). However, this process is not rigid—there are other context-specific factors as well ('Industry Attractiveness and Alternative Growth Avenues), based on the demands of the situation in which the organization is taking the decision to grow. It is hoped that the practical examples of Tata Nano and BFL offer an insight into how such growth has been achieved by two Indian organizations.

NOTES

1. Ansoff, I. H. (1957). 'Strategies for Diversification,' *Harvard Business Review*, 35 (5), pp. 113–24.
2. Hambrick, D. C. and Fredrickson, W. (2001). 'Are You Sure you have a Strategy?', *Academy of Management Executive*, 15 (4), pp. 48–59.
3. Bower, J.L., and Gilbert, C.G. (2005). *From Resource Allocation to Strategy*. New York: Oxford University Press.
4. Porter, M.E. (2008). 'The Five Competitive Forces that Shape Strategy', *Harvard Business Review*, 86 (1), pp. 78–93.
5. Laurie, D. L., Doz, Y. L, and Sheer, C. P. (2006). 'Creating New Growth Platforms', *Harvard Business Review*, 84 (5), pp. 80–90.
6. Excerpted from http://www.infibeam.co,/static/tata-nano.html on 13 August 2010.
7. Excerpted from http://finance.yahoo.com/family-home/article/102865/the-next-people-car on 13 August 2010.
8. Excerpted from http://www.kalganigroup.com/bhart frrge.asp on 13 August 2010.
9. Excerpted from http://www.bharatforge.com/ on 13 August 2010.

4

Growth through Vertical Integration

INTRODUCTION

Vertical integration as a tool for growth has been followed quite extensively. In this chapter, we attempt to first understand the meaning of vertical integration, which is deeply rooted in the direction organizations grow along its value chain—a detailed section on the value chain is included for subsequent discussion on growth using vertical integration.

THE CONCEPT OF VALUE CHAIN

In order to completely understand the competitive advantage of an organization, it isn't sufficient to look at it as a single entity. This trait resides in the various activities that it performs, like sourcing, designing, producing, packaging, marketing, distribution, and post-sales support. An organization can derive its advantage and achieve differentiation through any of these activities. For example, a strong sourcing plan for raw materials can go a long way in giving the organization significant cost advantage. Similarly, expertise in design can enable an organization to carve a niche for itself and gain a competitive advantage. Even information systems can be leveraged by an organization in service of differentiation.

The concept[1] of *value chain* enables one to divide an organization into its basic elements based on strategic importance. Such a dissection facilitates a deeper understanding of the costs incurred by these elements and explores the potential for differentiation. Competitive advantage can then be gained by focusing on improving the relevant elements derived from the above-mentioned analysis.

As an organization has a value chain, similarly, so do its suppliers as well as buyers. An organization's competitive advantage is also influenced by the coordination and synergies existing between its own value chain and that of its suppliers and buyers. For example, Toyota gains a significant competitive advantage because of its ability to synchronize its suppliers' value chain with its own (*Just-in-time philosophy*). Thus, the organization's value chain needs to be analysed in reference to the overall value system. Understanding the value system can provide insights into various strategic options like geographical or demographical segmentation, coalitions, diversification, etc.

Value Chain—The Key Idea

Every organization is an aggregation of various activities that are executed to source, design, produce, package, market, distribute, and support its products. All these activities can be visually represented using a value chain, as shown in Figure 4.1.[2] The value chain signifies the activities that an organization undertakes to offer value to its buyers. This value creation is integral to an organization's strategy. Enhancing value for the buyers whilst ensuring that the costs incurred in doing so are less than this value is a primary requirement of any strategy. A successful strategy results in a large positive difference between the value a product commands and the costs incurred in producing it, thus ensuring high profitability. The value of the product depends on the differentiation that the organization manages to create in its products, offered and the way it is delivered, which is ingrained in its own value chain.

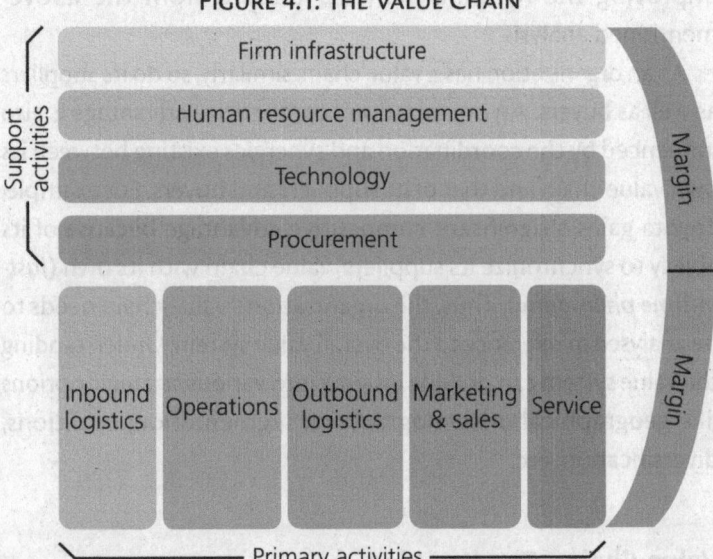

FIGURE 4.1: THE VALUE CHAIN

Source: Retrieved from http://en.wikipedia.org/wiki/value chain on 3 September 2010.

Value activities can be broadly divided into two categories, *primary activities* and *support activities*. Primary activities are those that are involved in the physical creation of the product, its distribution to the buyer, and sales support, whereas support activities are those that support the primary activities by providing purchase inputs, human resources, training, etc.

CONSTITUENTS OF THE VALUE CHAIN

Primary activities can be generically disaggregated into five categories: inbound logistics, operations, outbound logistics, sales and marketing, and service.

Inbound logistics deal with input sourcing and supply management, operations with the transformation of these inputs into the final product. Outbound logistics refer to the distribution of the product. Sales and marketing deal with the activities associated with buying cycles like advertising, sales promotion, pricing, etc. Service refers to the post-sales support provided to the buyer. The relative importance of each of these categories depends on the type of industry in which the organization is operating. For a generic manufacturing organization, operations would be critical, but for a distributor, logistics would be most important.

Support activities can be divided into four broad categories: procurement, human resource management, technology development, and firm infrastructure.

Procurement deals with the purchasing of the inputs used by the organization. Human resource management deals with the recruiting and reskilling activities undertaken by the organization. Technology development is concerned with new products and also improvement in existing production processes. Firm infrastructure includes activities related to general management, finances, government affairs, etc. Even support activities can be sources of competitive advantage to an organization. For example, for a technology firm, new product development is critical for its success but for an oil and gas firm, government relations are critical to obtain contracts. Each of these activities can be further disaggregated into sub-activities for further analysis, depenaling on the relative importance of the activities in the organizational context.

LINKAGES IN THE VALUE CHAIN

As mentioned earlier, the constituents of the value chain must be analysed as a system and not as independent activities. Rather, these are a set of extremely interdependent activities. For example, technological improvements may enhance the operational efficiency of a manufacturing organization. Promotional activities coordinated with warehouse inventory levels and logistics would ensure stock availability during heavy promotions. Understanding the linkages enables one to explore better coordination and optimally use the organization's resources. Linkages between the primary activities are quite intense and need to be carefully examined. For example, rigorous inspection of input quality reduces the quality assurance costs later in production. Coordinated delivery systems reduce warehousing costs and avoid inventory pile-up. Recognizing the importance of these linkages and gauging their current effective strength provides vital information that guides the organization's strategy. This strategy should be oriented towards further strengthening these linkages.

Vertical Linkages

Linkages between the organization's value chain and that of its suppliers and buyers also need to be analysed to gain competitive advantage. Output of suppliers' value chains influences the input to the organization. Better interaction between the inbound logistics of the organization and the suppliers' value chain reduces costs in terms of quality and inventory control. An organization can gain significant competitive advantage if it can optimize the two value chains. The supplier–organization relationship isn't a zero sum game but can result in a win for both if linkages are properly coordinated.

Similarly, linkages with the buyers' value chains are critical to an organization. Coordinated plans between the buyer and the organization can result in avoiding redundant expenditures and better value to the end-user. An organization can gain significant competitive advantage if linkages with its distribution channels are strong. Strong linkages result in faster and smoother rollout of new products with minimum inventory pile-up.

An organization must recognize the significance of these linkages for its functioning and devise its strategy to capitalize on them and gain sustainable competitive advantage.

WHAT IS VERTICAL INTEGRATION?

Based on our knowledge of value chains, we now know that vertical linkages are critical to an organization's sustainable competitive advantage. The concept of vertical integration defines the division of activities between an organization, its suppliers, distributors, and buyers. It can also be defined as a style of supply chain control. An organization may purchase its inputs directly from its suppliers or it may manufacture them itself. Or, instead of relying on a distributor network, the organization may set up one of its own. A higher degree of vertical integration would be when the organization takes up further value addition to its finished products (or input materials) to compete with its erstwhile buyers (or suppliers).

Vertical integration can be a strategic tool to counter various issues related to the value chain. It can be a tool to isolate an organization from external market fluctuations. Or it can be used to deal with an erratic partner (control supplier/buyer power). It can also be used as a strategy to enter into higher-value segments by venturing into post-processing of its product lines. But in general, it can be defined as a tool to control or exploit the advantages of an organization's value system.

Weak linkages between the organization's value chain and that of its upstream (suppliers) and downstream (channels and buyers) value chains may hinder the growth of the firm. For example, input material availability as required by the organization is dependent on the supplier–organization linkages. High supplier power may result in higher transaction costs for the organization. To control these fluctuations, vertical integration is one of the strategies available. An organization may also decide the degree of vertical integration. For example, an organization can internalize input material manufacturing while continuing to take supplier support for design and service.

Through vertical integration, an organization integrates the upstream or downstream value chains into its value chain. Thus, these value chains are converted into value activities for the organization, and post-integration, it is sufficient to optimize the organization's value chain to address the specific point of concern.

With vertical integration, an organization is expanding into relatively newer territories. Thus, it calls for resource mobilization to meet these new challenges. The existing market structure in these territories should also be weighed in during the decision-making process. Thus, a complete understanding of the organization's value system along with an intricate analysis of the new business foray is essential for a decision on vertical integration.

TYPES OF VERTICAL INTEGRATION

Backward Vertical Integration

When an organization controls some of its suppliers, it is termed as backward vertical integration. For example, an automobile manufacturing firm can acquire its parts manufacturers to streamline its supply side. But backward integration need not always be linked to reducing supply-side instability. An organization can also foray into its supply side if the profit margins in that value chain are significantly higher.

Forward Vertical Integration

When an organization controls some of its channels or buyers, it is termed as forward vertical integration. For example, an organization can acquire a trucking fleet to reduce distribution-related fluctuations. An organization may also enter the downstream product market into its buyers' activities and attain differentiation. Thus, even forward vertical integration can be used to stabilize the downstream value activities or enter into newer market segments.

Balanced Vertical Integration

When a firm involves itself in both its upstream and downstream value chains, it is termed as balanced integration.

Vertical integration as a tool can be a solution to many problems of an organization. Should an organization set up its own delivery system? Should an organization 'make' its inputs in-house or 'buy' its inputs or should it mix the two? Should an organization 'sell' its products or 'process' them further? Should an organization operate its own warehouse? To answer these questions with respect to vertical integration as an option, it is important to understand the merits and demerits of vertical integration. The following section details the relative advantages (opportunities) and disadvantages (challenges) of vertical integration.

BENEFITS/MERITS OF VERTICAL INTEGRATION

Vertical integration can provide many benefits or opportunities towards the growth of an organization. Better coordination and optimization of a given value system are the underlying cause for these benefits.

a. **Saving on transaction costs[3]:** Post-vertical integration, the affected activities change from a buyer–seller relationship to an internalized, interdependent activity relationship. The transaction costs may include handling costs, transportation costs, taxes, sales force costs, etc. This directly impacts the competitive advantage of the organization.

b. **Reduction of supply uncertainty[4]:** Internalizing input supply insulates the organization from problems arising due to supply variations. Shortage of input materials leads to idling of expensive facilities. In the absence of integration, entering into long-term contracts is an attempt by the organization to achieve the same result, but the organization also loses out on the possible gains of a positive supply-side fluctuation.

c. **Better in-house coordination:** Supply certainty doesn't guarantee optimal production routines. The difference in the objectives of two organizations (each wanting to maximize its profits) may result in suboptimal production schedules and inventory levels. In a vertically integrated firm, these schedules can be better optimized towards a common end, thus saving on costs.

d. **Technological flexibility:** With vertical integration, an organization gains valuable in-house flexibility to expedite implementation of technological changes and improvements into its processes. This flexibility adds to an organization's competitive advantage as it makes the organization agile and more adaptive to environmental changes.

e. **Entry barriers:** A vertically integrated business poses a significant deterrent to a prospective new entrant into the business due to the technological and managerial investments required. This is effective only if the integration constricts the new entrant from competing, in terms of resource supply or in terms of market availability.

f. **Capital investments:** An organization can undertake new investments in the upstream or downstream businesses post-integration, investments which the previous owners might have been reluctant to pursue. This enables an organization to develop substantial competitive advantage via differentiation.

g. **Gaining on upstream/downstream profit margins:** Entering into the upstream or downstream markets also enables the organization to gain on profit margins in those businesses. For example, supply-side integration might not only help the organization to smoothen supply-side fluctuations, but also enable the organization to use the additional capacity (if any) to sell the input materials in the open market.

CHALLENGES OR DEMERITS OF VERTICAL INTEGRATION

We discussed above the benefits that an organization can accrue out of growth tool of vertical integration. However, vertical integration also poses a set of unique challenges. Complete benefits of vertical integration would be diluted if the following challenges are not addressed sufficiently.

a. **Investment pressure:** Backward or forward integration places the organization under pressure to commit to investments in the new business arm to generate expected returns. So, unless the operational advantages exceed the investments demanded, the vertical integration move would be fraught with danger.

b. **Mismatched operating scales:** Even though vertical integration enables better in-house coordination, it poses the problem of managing input and output, as well as maintaining scale efficiency. As the two businesses might very well be operating under different scales owing to the industry dynamics prior to the integration, the combined business unit would now need to be either operated under inefficient scales or investments must be made to operate on a larger scale. Other solutions, like renting out part of the excess capacity or outsourcing, could be explored to harness the difference in scale.

c. **Reduced flexibility:** Although vertical integration increases flexibility in terms of technological changes, the same structure would be a deterrent for the organization when faced with a paradigm shift in technology. Investments in the upstream or downstream businesses could be rendered obsolete when faced with such a situation.

d. **Developing other core competencies**: Post-integration, an organization's vital resources are deployed towards developing core competencies in the new business arm. This can divert the organization's attention from continued improvement in its existing core competencies.

e. **Masking of inefficiencies:** Integration results in lengthening of the organization's value chains. Improper monitoring of these activities can result in masking of the inefficiencies in the new business arm due to lack of competition. For example, inefficiencies of suppliers are easily noticeable in the costs of the input materials because of the general availability of a competitive market. The organization could choose its supplier based on market knowledge. But post-integration, the new value system could very well mask the underperforming business arm. Monitoring of the newly integrated business system should be carried out as per industry norms to ensure that inefficiencies aren't camouflaged.

ILLUSTRATIONS

Illustration I: Reliance Industries

Reliance Industries is India's largest private sector conglomerate in terms of market value with an annual turnover exceeding USD44.6 billion[5] and USD3.6 billion in profits for the fiscal year ended March 2010. It is ranked 264th in the Fortune Global 500 and at 126th in the Fortune Global 2000 list. Reliance Industries is a brilliant example of innovative backward integration.

Reliance, under Dhirubhai Ambani, started off as a trading firm in 1959, primarily trading in yarns and fabrics. Heavy demand for rayon fabrics in India enabled Ambani to import rayon and generate healthy margins. When the demand shifted to nylon, Reliance shifted its import focus to nylon. The entrepreneur found that there was a deficiency of good quality fabrics for export, so, in a backward integration move, Ambani set up manufacturing operations for nylon fabrics in 1966 to gain from the significant market gap. As nylon lost ground to polyester, the Indian government relaxed regulations, allowing import of polyester against export of nylon fabrics. Ambani expanded operations in this field and began importing polyester. The organization leveraged import entitlements to upgrade its manufacturing facilities for both the value-add of imported yarn as well as world-class fabric manufacturing. With a shift in public policy, Reliance looked to the domestic market, and with its high quality manufacturing facilities, it gained complete control over the Indian domestic market. In one of its forward integration moves, Reliance entered into the retail distribution of its fabrics, and by 1980 it owned more than twenty retail stores in India and over 1000 franchised outlets. With a government restriction on loom installations for larger organizations, Reliance increased its capacity by procuring grey fabrics from small-scale power looms.

In 1982[6], Reliance integrated backward again by entering the business of manufacturing polyester filament yarn (PFY). Domestic demand was higher than the domestic supply and the shortfall was met by imports. Ambani had visited facilities around the world to observe yarn production and found inefficiencies in production processes. Considering that one of its major inputs was PFY and that the cost of those inefficiencies would be directly reflected on his cost of inputs, he considered this to be an extremely strategic move. Reliance installed huge PFY building facilities by buying the technology from Du Pont, intending to create stiff barriers for competition as well as stimulating demand rather than following it. In 1984, Reliance expanded its polyester business by setting up manufacturing facilities for polyester staple fibre (PSF).

Reliance backward integrated further into manufacture of fibre intermediates PTA, LAB, and MEG. The firm kept its focus on both domestic and export markets to ensure that the higher capacities were well utilized. In 1983, Reliance horizontally expanded into manufacturing high density polyethylene (PE) and poly vinyl chloride (PVC). Between 1989 and 1992, it integrated backwards by setting up manufacturing facilities for input materials for LAB, directly from kerosene with N-paraffin as the intermediate, and for PTA, manufactured from paraxylene. It set up an ethylene cracker complex, which would provide the ethylene needed for the manufacture of PE, PVC, and MEG. It also set up a unit to produce ethylene dicholoride, a feedstock for PVC. In 1992, Reliance increased its presence in the polypropylene and polyethylene production business by commissioning new plants. In another move backwards, it obtained a licence for setting up a 9 MT refinery. This refinery would meet its feedstock requirements of naphtha for its paraxylene plant. It also entered into retail distribution of the refinery's range of products. To complete the backward integration, Reliance entered into the oil and gas exploration business by bidding for oilfields and has been successful in discovering natural gas reserves in the Krishna-Godavari basin off the coast of Andhra Pradesh near Visakhapatnam.

This backward integration has been a judicious mix of supply considerations and exploiting profit margins of upstream value chains. Investment requirements for these new businesses was carefully thought through and executed, and resources were utilized optimally for Reliance to emerge as a market leader in the entire value chain. A vertically integrated firm in a core business with substantial investments in capacity thwarts potential entrants and enables a firm to maintain its competitive advantage.

Illustration II: Bowmar Calculators

Bowmar Calculators was essentially an organization engaged in the manufacture of LED displays.[7] In a strategic move to vertically integrate, it entered the downstream value chain to add value to its existing products and started making calculators in 1970–1[8]. The organization sourced integrated circuit chips from its suppliers and focused on the calculator business. Bowmar soon emerged as the market leader in pocket calculator production. In the mid-1970s, this lucrative business attracted competitors and its suppliers found it easy to vertically integrate with their technological ability and financial supremacy. Bowmar found itself unable to compete in the ensuing price war and decided to integrate backwards into production of semiconductor chips to ensure supply and reduce cost. This move was ill-fated for many reasons. First, the core competency needed in the semiconductor business was much different from the competencies that Bowmar possessed. The investment needed in the new business was beyond the financial resources at Bowmar's disposal. More importantly, the semiconductor industry was already operating under heavy overcapacity leading to erosion of profit margins. The technology flexibility also compromised Bowmar's core business of calculator manufacturing, rendering the organization bankrupt. The organization had an innovative product but failed to sustain its competitive advantage due to its overdependence on the suppliers to maintain it. The foray into the new semiconductor venture was too late to salvage its competitive advantage.

Illustration III: De Beers

The De Beers family of companies[9] is involved in the mining, processing, and trading of diamonds. Throughout the twentieth century, De Beers manipulated the diamond market by controlling supply and forming cartels. De Beers had control of the biggest diamond mines in South Africa, giving it a significant market power. However, with the discovery of newer mines in other parts of the world and high incentive for other diamond firms to defect from the cartel, De Beers found its market position at risk. It consolidated its trading arm by setting up technological facilities aimed at the quality control of diamonds. In a strategic move, De Beers entered into the downstream segment and began to manufacture diamond jewellery. It tied up with Louis Vuitton Moet Hennessy to establish an independent De Beers diamond jewellery company. The move was successful, as De Beers had a strong brand recall and the core competencies required in the new business venture weren't radically different from its existing business. Also, the retail business held higher profit margins and De Beers was well positioned to exploit it to sustain its competitive advantage.

CONCLUSION

Vertical integration brings with it both benefits and challenges. The competitive structure, regulation mechanisms, criticality of the particular business to the organization, business scale, core competencies demanded, investment needs, etc., all play an important role in the decision-making process. For example, if the amount of input material required from a supplier isn't sufficient to produce the input efficiently, vertical integration wouldn't be attractive unless there exists an attractive enough market for the additional capacity. Similarly, if regulation mechanisms enforce strict monitoring over the formation of contracts between business units, vertical integration might make sense, provided all other relevant conditions are satisfied. An organization must also take into consideration the new competitors it may face in light of is new venture and ensure that this set of organizations does not conflict with its existing collaborators.

Capital and resource investments must be carefully estimated before the integration venture. The degree of integration must also be finalized prior to the integration. A half-hearted attempt at integration might very well leave the organization in a 'neither here, nor there' position resulting in erosion of the pre-integration competitive advantage as well as a drain on precious capital resources. Scale issues must also be addressed prior to the venture as these may place additional demands on capital. Post-integration analysis of the business unit must be unbiased and of industry standards to gain an accurate insight into the success of the venture. Other options like long-term contracts, alliances, joint ventures, relocation of facilities, etc. which might provide similar benefits but with different drawbacks must be carefully considered before going ahead with vertical integration.

NOTES

1. Porter, M. (1985). *Competitive Advantage: Creating and Sustaining Superior Performance*, New York: The Free press.
2. Excerpted from http://in.wikipedia.org/wiki/valwe chain on 2 September 2010.
3. Sebire, G. (2010). 'Accelerate your reverse logistics', *MHD Supply Chain Logistics*, May–June, p. 44.

4. Buzzel, R.D. (1983). 'Is vertical interation profitable?' *Harvard Business Review*, 61(1), pp. 92–102.

5. Excerpted from http://www.ril.com/html/aboutus. html on 2 September 2010.

6. Excerpted from http://www.ril.com/html/aboutus/majormilestones. html on 2 September 2010.

7. Excerpted from http://www.rintagecalculators.com/html/bouemar calculator. html on 30 August 2010.

8. Excerpted from http://www.litmieng.com.ac.uk/dmg/tares/louemar. html on 30 August 2010.

9. Excerpted from www.debeers.com on 2 September 2010.

5

Growth through Disruptive Innovation

INTRODUCTION

Disruptive innovation has evolved as an important tool for organizational growth. However, readers should not confuse the phenomenon of disruptive innovation with research and development. Often, disruptive innovation starts with simple ideas being commercialized as a simple product offering targeted at a small segment of customers. However, with time, this value proposition engulfs a substantial portion of the industry. In this chapter, we discuss the role of disruptive innovation in deciding such a fascinating trajectory for an organization.

DISRUPTIVE INNOVATION—THE KEY IDEA

Let us first understand the essence of disruptive innovation. Only then will we be able to appreciate its relevance as a growth tool for organizations. Let us describe a situation that will help us understand the concept of disruptive innovation.[1] Suppose an organization comes up with a value proposition (product/service) that is not considered mainstream in the industry. This value proposition is aimed at another segment altogether, in that targeted customers are not the key users of mainstream products available in that industry. These customers are at the lower strata of society. However, over time, this value proposition graduates to win upmarket customers as well, in a way that dislodges existing players from the industry. This phenomenon, by virtue of which a new organization comes up with a value proposition which alters the rules of the game for the industry, is called disruptive innovation.

Disruptive innovation is an excellent tool for growth when an organization wants to enter an industry that is dominated by a few big players with significantly evolved products, when this aspiring organization lacks the financial muscle to take these big players head-on with said products; or maybe, even if the organization has the strength, a direct clash isn't desired. Products of this new entrant organization are aimed at customers with low purchasing power. Over time, these products are adopted by customers in the higher strata of society.

Diametrically opposite to the phenomenon of disruption innovation is the idea of sustaining innovation—the phenomenon of developing incremental features in the existing product offering. In the absence of disruption, it is generally the big players in an industry that win the game of sustaining innovation. Over time, sustaining innovation leads to marked improvement in the value proposition. This tempts the organization to target the value proposition to the upper strata of society for better margins. As a result, a vacuum is created at the lower end of the market, and often it is through this gap that some organizations begin their disruptive innovation.

GROWTH STRATEGIES USING DISRUPTIVE INNOVATION

When a new idea comes up, the management of an organization will try to develop it towards a commercial end. This can take the form of either sustaining innovation or disruptive innovation. Though profits are higher in the long run by following the path of disruption, organizations often shy away from it. This is because of high uncertainty and ambiguity. Such apprehension tends to result in pushing an existing product towards improvement, ultimately leading to sustaining innovation. However, there may be organizations dedicated to pursuing growth in a specific business context through disruptive innovation[2]. This section is dedicated to the two routes that such organizations can take for growth.

Route I: Developing a New Market Altogether

To begin with, it is always better for an organization to aim a product at a set of customers who don't buy the existing and established alternative products. It is always easier to make a new customer rather than trying to lure customers away from other big organizations. Prospective customers should be the ones who have always wanted to own the product/service, as they find utility in the value proposition. However, their ability to own that product/service has been constrained for one reason or the other. This may be either because of lack of money to own the product, or maybe the lack of the customers' ability to use the product. Needless to say, if the product is to be such that customers are able to use it with ease, then the product should be simple enough. There is another important thing that 'disruptive' organizations should keep in mind. The product should address the active need of target customers. There is no point in introducing a product which is not needed, irrespective of how fantastic it is. Assimilation of a new product will be fast if customers need it and if there is no available alternative in the market prior to launch.

Route II: Introducing New Rules-of-the Game in an Existing Market

Sometimes, the offering of an organization is such that it has to be targeted to existing customers. Since the value proposition cannot be rolled out to new customers, the strategy mentioned above fails. However, non-conformance to the conditions mentioned in Route I should not be a sufficient reason for organizations to abandon their pursuit of growth through disruptive innovation. There are ways of targeting the customers in existing markets as well. However, this requires an organization to check a few things first, to understand the feasibility of the disruptive-innovation-based growth pursuit.

For one, existing products should offer features that are more than what customers want. To analyse if such is the case or not, the first step will be to segregate the customers into segments. If we see that even after introduction of new features in the product (and corresponding increase in the product price), customers across all the segments stick to existing consumption, we can say that the features are not more than what existing customers want. However, if there are a few segments which cease consumption after feature enhancement, then we can be certain that these segments are neither interested in the new features nor are they ready to pay the increased price. An organization can offer products with simple features, targeted to these segments which have stopped using products of existing players. This automatically puts a cap on the price that can be charged. This threshold price, along with the basic profit margin necessary for business sustenance, determines the ceiling of cost within which the scaled-down products will have to be produced and distributed.

Also, we need to appreciate that the existence of such an opportunity is not necessarily sufficient for success. Organizations should have a business model in place, detailing how the business proposition will be executed. The components of such a disruptive business plan would include cost details, distribution mechanisms, and value chains. It is understandable that by offering products with basic features, margins would be low. But a low margin should not impede such disruptive businesses, as the fixed assets to be deployed for running the business are also low. Hence, the rules of the game in an existing market are altered altogether with the introduction of a new business model by entrant organizations.

BUILDING DISRUPTIVE INNOVATION CAPABILITY

We saw earlier how a new organization with relatively low resources is able to capture market share using disruptive innovation. Smaller, or for that matter, younger organizations have the inherent ability to develop disruptive innovation capability as the basis of their agility. Though smaller organizations are agile, it is not completely beyond the scope of larger organizations to engage in disruptive innovation. Let us discuss here the routes that these larger organizations can take to develop these capabilities.

Route I: In-house Capability Development

If an organization wants to develop disruptive innovation internally, then it requires some people to think outside the traditional thought process of the organization. This is because to develop such disruption-based capabilities, big organizations need to alter the very paradigm of their thought process. Employees entrusted with the task of developing such capabilities need to think and act very differently from other line managers. This is only possible if these employees are brought together to form a different team, insulated from other day-to-day operations with the key objective being the development of disruptive innovation capabilities. It is only when the team members are focused entirely on this cause that such capabilities are possible to be created.

Route II: Capability Development through Alliances

The Route I (as well as Route III) of developing capabilities are organic in nature. But there are times when the capabilities that the organization seeks to build are available in the market with other organizations. At times, it might be advisable to 1) either collaborate with these other entities towards a learning ambience, 2) or simply acquire those organizations and the desired capabilities will then come within the ambit of the organization seeking penetration. There are two important things that managers need to consider when taking this route to capability development. One, that it is critical to be able to correctly assess if the other organization (with which alliance is targeted) has the sought capabilities or not. If there is any error in such an assessment, then this move can cause a lot of trouble for the organization. Two, the assessment should bring out the exact roots where these capabilities are embedded. Otherwise, learning objective will fail miserably. If the other organization posseses the necessary capabilities and this organization is acquired, integration post-acquisition will greatly help the acquirer organization.

Route III: Special Purpose Vehicle

There are times when the values and processes of a big organization are such that they are aligned strongly with the requirements of a big business. In the presence of such internal dynamics, it would be impossible for a disruptive innovation project to see the light of day. This is because of the inherent nature of such a project, which is aimed at an emerging and uncertain market with a very small business to begin with. In such cases, the disruptive innovation project should be accorded a different organizational status. This will distance the project from the inertia of the organization's conventional values. By being a different entity, it won't have to compete, time and again, with the line functions of the organization for resource allocation. But there is a catch here. In its infancy, this special purpose vehicle should be given the due parenting by the CEO of the parent organization. Only then will the team be motivated for its success.

SUSTAINING VERSUS DISRUPTIVE INNOVATION—THE TRADE-OFF

The sections above have emphasized the fact that creating disruptive innovation capabilities is very different from sustaining innovation capabilities—to the extent that it is often felt these capabilities are conflicting in nature, and managing both these within a single organizational boundary may be impossible. Managerial resources available to an organization are indeed a constraint, and this creates a challenge for an organization to design a delicate balance between sustaining and disruptive innovations[3].

On a day-to-day basis, sustaining innovation definitely receives greater managerial attention. To ensure that disruptive innovation pursuits don't take a backseat, an organization should allocate specific resources, at the beginning of the budgetary allocation itself, for such pursuits in the middle of a business cycle (more so for an organization seeking ambitious growth trajectory). Any request for resources to kick-start or continue a disruptive innovation pursuit is bound to be turned down since such pursuits have small, uncertain markets to begin with and fall short of the traditional way of measuring success of a business. So, a sustaining innovation project will always get priority than one of disruptive innovation if there is a clash for organizational resources. But an organization needs to understand that this is not a zero sum game. As a result, there should be separate funds for the specific purpose of encouraging disruption-related projects. This will ensure that neither sustaining nor disruptive innovation pursuits feel that the other is cannibalizing required resources.

This brings us to another equally important measure that organizations should take to ensure that disruptive innovation pursuits are not compromised. We have been saying, time and again, that business growth through disruptive innovation follows a very different trajectory altogether. By their very nature, these innovation projects germinate in emerging markets with high uncertainty. It would be incorrect to measure these projects the way managers evaluate traditional ones—financial matrices, period-over-period growth, market presence, etc. will all go wrong. This is not to say there should be no performance evaluation of these projects at all, but there needs to be a qualitative assessment of these pursuits. Since these disruptive innovation projects operate under uncertainty, the assessment should involve evaluation of the assumptions made by the managers and their relevance thereof. Also, an attempt should be made to understand how comprehensive these assumptions are, and whether they address all the contingencies that can arise in the business environment.

ILLUSTRATIONS

Illustration I: Apple iPod/ iTunes

Apple, Inc. is considered iconic when it comes to product development. This example attempts to explain the way in which iTunes may be considered a disruptive innovation. The iPod was launched in 2001, a year in which Apple's global market share of personal computers was around three percent. The iPod is a device where customers load digital songs for subsequent listening. It is important to point out here that at the time there were other digital music players, such as MP3 players, available in the market which could serve similar utility for customers. However, Apple had the foresight to encourage iPod customers to use the Internet. Along with the launch of the iPod, Apple also launched iPod Lounge, a website owned by Apple wherein iPod users could design customized covers and accessories for their music device and send suggestions to the organization. Simultaneously, Apple launched iTunes. iTunes is software used to play and organize digital music. Apple ensured that iTunes was bundled with each iPod. iTunes ensured that songs available in common formats such as MP3 could not be played on the iPod. These songs had to be converted to an iPod-specific format using the iTunes[4] interface to be played.

Two years on, in 2003, Apple launched the iTunes Music Store. This was an Internet-based interface through which iPod users could load songs onto their music player. Songs were available in the iTunes Music Store for a nominal cost of USD 0.99[5].

If we look at the sequencing of product introduction by Apple, it is clear that the iPod was not a disruptive innovation. Products with similar output features existed in the market, as discussed earlier. It is the bundling with iTunes that gave Apple the disruptive edge. It changed the very business model of the industry (remember Route III mentioned above). Because of iTunes, iPod users were locked-in and had to purchase songs from the iTunes store. By previously encouraging customers to use iPod Lounge, a perception in the market had already been built that iPod users had to be educated in Internet use. It was not a very daunting task for Apple to lead iPod users to the iTunes Music Store to purchase music.

Illustration II: Nintendo's Wii

This case illustrates the introduction of disruptive innovation in the video game industry, wherein a relatively smaller player grows (using the tool of disruptive innovation, of course) to overtake stable bigwigs. Fusajiro Yamauchi founded Nintendo[6] in 1951. Prior to this, he had ventured into the business of playing cards in 1889[7]. Nintendo continued to manufacture and sell playing cards until 1970, when the organization began making video games and electronic toys, after which it entered the United States market, making and marketing video games and enhancements.

The year 2000 was a landmark year for the video game industry, given that all the three major players launched new products. Previously, Nintendo was the market leader in video gaming. However, with the launch of Sony's PlayStation2, Nintendo lost this coveted position. PS2 outsold its competitors, including Microsoft's Xbox and Nintendo's GameCube. Sony and Microsoft continued to enhance their products by adding new features, but with the appointment of Satoru Iwata as President of Nintendo in 2002, the organization decided to take a very different route to growth.

Nintendo observed that in Japan the customer base of the video game industry was in decline. This may be attributed to new variants of the products being very complicated. The product features were more than what many segments of customers wanted. Even in the segment that remained, Sony and Microsoft continued to launch new product enhancements. Given this current industry paradigm, Nintendo decided to take a different path altogether (remember Route I mentioned above). It realized that there is a huge market for non-gamers as well. There were segments of the existing customer base which slowly ceased to buy video games, the ones with increased enhancements as well as price. Nintendo decided to target these two segments.[8]There was definitely uncertainty, as new product introduction was not the sure shot mantra for success. Also, since this would be an emerging market, traditional measures of performance might give a gloomy picture. Despite all this, Nintendo launched the Wii—a revolution in itself. Here was a video game system with games that could be played with a simple wand-like controller. There was no complex wiring or controls to be manoeuvred. The movement of the controller was detected by the screen's motion detectors, translating these motions into gaming action. Needless to say, this was an instant hit, and within a year of Wii's launch, the market value of Nintendo tripled.

Apart from Route I, there is another element of the Wii strategy that we need to discuss. Prior to the launch of Wii in 2006[9], the organization had moved very cautiously in capturing the new market segment. It was taking baby steps so that any wrong move didn't prove disastrous. For example, Nintendo developed and launched a new hand-held gaming device called double screen

(DS) in 2004. This was the first step towards a simplified product, and this had a touchscreen. Customers could even write on the screen using a stylus. There was no need for an array of buttons or a joystick to play games. Next, a Wi-Fi connection was launched, as a result of which DS users could play with other players on a particular network. Based on these steps, the Wii was finally launched in 2006.

Illustration III: Tata Nano

Tata Nano is the Rs 1 lakh car released by Tata Motors in 2008. It was made available to customers from 2009, and is considered the cheapest car in the world. This car was launched against the backdrop of intense competition in the Indian automobile industry. Not only were existing national players coming up with a new range of cars, but foreign organizations had started setting up shop. Previously, the Indica V2 (specifically the diesel variant), a product of Tata Motors, was considered an outright success with a substantial market share. For more details of the Nano venture, readers are advised to refer to illustrations in Chapter 3.

Tata Nano was targeted more towards two-wheeler owners (elements of Route I). This led to the creation of an entirely new segment. This market did not exist earlier, given the unaffordability of even the basic variants of other automobiles. Also, this market was initially uncertain and at a nascent stage. All these factors qualify this move of Tata Motors as one of disruptive innovation.

CONCLUSION

For an organization that aspires to enter a market already occupied by strong incumbents, disruptive innovation seems to be a key driver of success. The organization may enter by creating a new market altogether, or may create a new business model in a specific industry set-up, thereby altering the rules of playing the competitive game altogether. Both these require an organization to have an appetite for uncertainty, as forecasting the future of an emerging market is a near impossibility. Also, the two alternatives to disruptive innovation require an organization to be agile. This puts large organizations at a disadvantage when it comes to exploiting the tool of disruptive innovation for growth. However, we suggest that relevant capabilities can be built by these organizations as well, either in-house or by creating a special purpose vehicle, or even by alliancing with (or merging/acquiring) another organization with the requisite capabilities. While promoting disruptive innovation, organizations should keep in mind that a subtle balance needs to be maintained between disruptive and sustaining innovation. There should be specific resource allocation, *ex ante*, for disruptive innovation projects, and these projects should be measured along unconventional qualitative performance measures. The three real life examples are taken to understand how these concepts of disruptive innovation unfold in organizations.

NOTES

1. The idea of disruptive innovation was first championed by Professor Clayton Christensen (excerpted) from http://www.clayton christensen.com/disruptive_innovation.html on 20 August 2010.

2. Christensen, C. M., Johnson, M., and Rigby, D.K. (2002). 'Foundations for Growth: How to identify and build disruptive new business', *MIT Sloan Management Review*, 43 (3), pp. 22–31.

3. Anthony, S.D. and Christensen, C. M. (2005). 'Innovator's Insights: Can you disrupt and sustain at the same time?', *Harvard Management Update*, 10(2), pp. 3–4.

4. Excerpted from http://www.apple.com/itunes/what-is/on 20 August 2010.

5. Excerpted from http://news.cnet.com/will-iTunes-make-Apple-shine/2100-1041 3-5092559.html on 20 August 2010.

6. Excerpted from http://nintendo.wikia.cona/wiki/fusajiro.Yamauchi on 21 August 2010.

7. Excerpted from http://www.nndb.com/peole/597/000206976/ on 21 August 2010.

8. Excerpted from http://wii.ign.com/launchguide/hardware1 on 20 August 2010.

9. Excerpted from http://en.wikipedia.org/wiki/wii on 21 August 2010.

Growth through Diversification

INTRODUCTION

This chapter is dedicated to gaining an understanding of diversification as a tool for organizational growth. Stakes are high, and such a move can make or break the prospects of an organization to prosper. After all, the higher the risk, the higher the return. Herein, we will try to understand the ways in which associated risks can be hedged by employing robust management tools of a priori analysis before any move is undertaken. We begin with an understanding of the concept of diversification. It is important for us to arrive at a common understanding, given the different ways different schools of thought define it. We illustrate three typical cases: the Tata Group, Microsoft, and Videocon to show how different organizations in different contexts have created and emerged as leaders by growing through the route of diversification.

UNDERSTANDING DIVERSIFICATION

Definition and Nature—The Key Concept

Diversification as a growth tool is generally considered to be a major decision for any organization. If executed with sufficient rigour, this tool can often lead to sweeping changes in the stature. Hence, before we embark on our journey to understand the way in which diversification can lead to enhanced business, it is important that we arrive at a common platform on what we mean by the concept of diversification.

Traditionally, 'diversification' was understood in terms of the presence of an organization in different products or markets. It was the combination of such presence, which would give an organization the image of being diversified. To understand how one product would be considered 'different' from another, to suggest if the organization was truly diversified, the Standard Industry Classification (SIC) was used as a heuristic.[1] Each four-digit SIC code, as designed by the United States government, represents an industry. By using this SIC code, one can understand the number of industries in which an organization's businesses are present: the more the count, the greater the degree of diversification. Though widely accepted, there are a few inherent flaws in this method. One of the most prominent is that it does not factor in the extent to which an organization's businesses or markets are related or overlap. This is a serious problem, as relatedness in business can often be a result of similar alternative growth avenues (for a detailed understanding of the concept of 'Alternative Growth Avenues', please refer to Chapter 3).

Subsequent research came up with a more holistic way of understanding diversification. Apart from considering the number of businesses under one organization, this approach would also consider which businesses were related. In this new approach, the presence in businesses per se is not very important—more important is the sales contribution of each business to the overall organization. Before embarking on the journey of understanding the new definition of diversification, it is important to understand one of its typical dimensions, namely, relatedness. It is important for the reader to understand the way in which relatedness is constructed. Businesses are related based on qualification on either (or all) of the said qualitative conditions.

▶ One, the products/services of these businesses use similar production technologies.
▶ Two, the development and production of the products/services of these businesses benefit from similar research.
▶ Three, the businesses are present in similar markets or the products/services exploit similar channels of sales.

There are three dimensions that, when taken together, define the diversification of an organization: 1) the number of businesses in which the organization is present; 2) the revenues of these different businesses to overall organizational revenues; and 3) the degree of relatedness of these businesses.

TYPES OF DIVERSIFIED ORGANIZATIONS

We can arrive at different organizational forms of diversification by altering the three dimensions that we just mentioned. These differences in the organizational forms essentially reflect the different routes that organizations take to grow by following the strategy of diversification. These may be a bit difficult to comprehend, but it was decided to include this given the acceptance of such classification amongst both academics and managers. A few organizational forms[2] that can take shape are 1) organizations with presence in multiple businesses, but a sizeable portion of the revenues (around or more than 95 percent) being contributed by a single business => 'single business'; 2) organizations with presence in multiple businesses, but a substantial proportion of the revenues (around or more than 70 percent) being contributed by a business or businesses that uses the same raw materials (such businesses are largely a result of joint products and/or by-products of same production process) => 'dominant vertical'; 3) organizations with businesses that have up to a substantial portion of the revenues (less than 70 percent) not being contributed by the group of even somewhat related businesses => 'unrelated businesses'; 4) organizations with presence in multiple areas, such that development and subsequent success of those businesses is based on an organization's common pool of skills and resources => 'related businesses'.

CHECKLIST FOR SUCCESS THROUGH DIVERSIFICATION

As we mentioned earlier, diversification is a big move for any organization, and at times, the success or failure of such a move can not only dictate the entire future trajectory of the organization, but also decide if the organization survives or not. With stakes that high, such moves should be based on an in-depth judicious business analysis.[3] Below are seven conditions, and an organization should concur with all of these to succeed in diversification.

Institutional Dynamics

The organization that decides to diversify should first understand the institutional framework of the industry/country. It is quite possible that the diversification move makes perfect sense for the organization, but the institutional mechanism might not support such a move. If there are regulators present, then their activeness decides such institutional context. In absence of active regulators, it is generally the incumbent organizations that dictate the industry institutional framework.

Value Addition in New Business

An organization needs to understand and articulate the capabilities of its current businesses. This can be done by assessing its strengths compared to industry competitors. Such an internal assessment of strengths will help managers understand how they will be able to add further value to the proposed business.

Gap in Benchmarked Capabilities

Having understood the in-house capabilities that the organization can use towards the betterment of the proposed move, the next step is to assess the additional capabilities that are required by the enterprise to succeed in the new market. After all, it is imperative that the organization possesses all the capabilities required to succeed in the new market; if the move is made with only a few of the needed capabilities, then failure or mediocrity in the new venture is certain.

Fulfilment of the Capability Gap

Once the gap in organizational strengths is identified, the next immediate step should be an action plan based on exercising how to ensure elimination of gaps. This is a difficult step, and often requires an increase in organizational expenditure on development of the capabilities under scrutiny. At the same time, capability development is often a time-consuming process—in-house development may not be possible if the opportunity for diversification is to be grabbed. Possibilities to fill the gap may arise by way of purchasing the capabilities from another player, or through collaboration. And there is another way: an organization may change the rules of the game that exist in the industry altogether. Such a change in paradigm will ensure that capabilities available to competitors become obsolete, nullifying their competitive position.

Understanding Capability Sets

Often, while executing the previous stages, an organization fails to see how certain capabilities can lend to competitive advantage by coexistence. If these capabilities are taken out of context and not together, they have a tendency to fail. It is, thus, important that the organization realizes that some of the necessary capabilities are a result of dynamic relationships with others, and the organization should take steps to effectively redeploy these in the new situations.

Expected Performance in the New Pursuit

An organization will decide to grow using diversification only if management feels that this pursuit will lead to a reasonably competitive position for it in the new market. If an organization does not plan, in advance, to be a clear winner in the new pursuit, then there are high chances that it may actually not even gain a foothold in the new market.

For an organization to ensure that it wins, it should see if it qualifies for the acid test of VRIN.[4] First of all, the strengths of the organization in the new pursuit should be 'valuable', that is the strengths should help the organization to make strategic moves that result in improvement in efficiency and/or effectiveness. Second, these strengths should be 'rare', that is the strengths should be so unique that they are not commonly found in competitors of that industry. Also, these capabilities should not be such that other players are able to source them from alternative places. If our organization has resources which are found amongst other competitors, this cannot be a source of competitive advantage. Third, these resources should be 'inimitable', that is other organizations should not be able to easily copy these strengths. This requires the strengths to be such that they are derived from a combination of resources, such that there is a particular way the resources are aligned with each other. The way this alignment takes place decides the degree of inimitability. There may be other sources of inimitability as well. For example, if the resource development is a function of time, then competitors won't be able to copy them. Another example can be a situation where competitors are not able to decipher the exact causality of these strengths—in such a situation, competitors will not be able to identify the actual resources lending themselves to the strengths of the organization. Finally, the strengths should be 'non-substitutable'; this means resources should not have readily available substitutes. This condition is as important as the three mentioned above, because even if organizational strengths are not imitable by competitors, the resources leading to such strengths might have available substitutes. Competitors may choose to make use of those substitutes to derive similar strengths, thereby nullifying the edge an organization may have been enjoying after diversification.

Expected Learning—A Priori

Good managers understand that diversification is not an end in itself, but a means of achieving an end—the end being organizational growth. As a result, the plan to diversify is just a move, to be followed by other such moves in the market. Given this, a top management team will try to understand the expected learning that the proposed diversification will offer. It is only if the organization is gaining a lot by way of know-how (and better still, know-why) that diversification makes sense. On the other hand, if the proposed diversification offers only stand-alone financial sense, without the learning necessary for further moves in other new businesses, then the organization should probably seek to investigate other options of diversification.

There is another level where learning can take place. Managers should also try to evaluate the relevance of new learning and whether it can also better existing businesses. It is always possible that the proposed diversification is not leading to specific learning for subsequent business moves. But the prospects of the expected learning in current businesses may be substantial. If such a benefit is anticipated, then we understand that organizations should consider the planned diversification all the more.

BENEFITS OF DIVERSIFICATION—AN EMERGING MARKET CONTEXT[5]

It has been found, based on practical illustrations, that emerging markets are such that well-diversified organizations have a higher propensity to succeed. We discuss the reasons in the subsequent sub-section. First, let us have a clear understanding of the meaning of an emerging market, as understood in management parlance.

Defining an Emerging Market

There are many ways of classifying markets. Put simply, a market is defined by the ease with which buyers and sellers reach out to each other. The ease of such transactions is often conditioned by the presence of institutional mechanisms, which ensure fairness. These mechanisms may vary in their degree of evolution, and this defines market characteristics. In the case of emerging markets, there are many shortcomings in the efficacy of these institutions. Here, we discuss a few such shortcomings for a better understanding of the characteristics of an emerging market.

The first problem is the lack of information transfer. If there are buyers and sellers, then an efficient market will ensure exhaustive information about the requirements and offerings of buyers to sellers, and vice versa. However, in emerging markets, such a free flow of information is missing. The lack of sufficient and reliable information makes it difficult for buyers and sellers to trust each other, making transactions inefficient.

The second problem associated with emerging markets is the presence of industrial laws guided more by political and populist considerations rather than economic ones. In advanced economies, we find the policy of 'hire and fire' that organizations follow; also, there is no legislative intervention when organizations follow such rules for their sustenance. But the situation is different in emerging economies. There are regulations against layoffs. This reduces organizational agility when it comes to quick movements from one business to another, especially when it comes to unexpected business opportunities.

There is another problem in less developed markets. To understand it, let us first of all agree that an organization has different stakeholders, and it is the interaction between these stakeholders that help the organization prosper. These stakeholders can be suppliers of raw materials, contractors, employees, channel partners (through whom the end-products/services are distributed), and customers. Transactions with these stakeholders often require the organization to enter into legal or even covert contracts with the parties concerned. Now, contract enforcement may require presence of redressal mechanisms, such as ombudsman (quasi-judiciary) and the judiciary. Emerging markets are characterized by their inefficient judicial systems. This makes appeals to the judiciary, in the case of contract non-enforcement, a tedious and time-consuming task on the part of the organization.

Benefits of Diversification in an Emerging Market

Having understood what an emerging market is, let us now understand the reasons why well-diversified organizations have an advantage over others who follow a focused strategy. Efficient institutional mechanisms are a prerequisite for the success of businesses in any market. But in emerging markets, there are inherent problems (as discussed above). Diversified organizations, by virtue of their being present in multiple businesses spread across numerous territories, can take advantage of gaps in institutional mechanisms. Let us now look at a few ways in which diversified organizations have a better grip over markets in emerging situations.

First, in an emerging market, the flow of information and communication is restricted. As a result, it is difficult for a new organization to inform potential customers of its value. At the same time, it is equally difficult for potential customers to authenticate the claims of this new organization about its product/service, and in the case of dissonance post-purchase, seek reprise (due to tedious judiciary processes). In light of this, if an already established, credible, well-diversified organization enters a new market domain, potential customers have a tendency to trust the product/service's value based on a diversified organization's previous track record.

Second, emerging markets are also characterized by lack of proper reporting mechanisms for organizations. This results in making it difficult for financial institutions (such as banks and venture capitalists) to fund a single-business company. Just like customers, investors will look at the credibility of an organization before giving any loans. Well-diversified organizations can always use their past track record as credit for future performance on a new project. Investors also feel more secure giving loans to organizations that have businesses spread out. There is another benefit that diversified organizations have with respect to raising capital. Diversified organizations can channel funds from one business line to another; if there are a few businesses that are doing well and have surplus funds, these can be used to finance new diversification moves without seeking outside capital.

Third, just like scarcity of product communication and capital disbursement, there is a lack of skilled personnel in an emerging market. When emerging markets begin opening up, there is a sudden increase in manpower (skilled in specific vocations), but the educational system is yet to be able to supply all the necessary training. Diversified organizations can reduce dependability on external skilled workforce by conducting professional development workshops in-house. This is generally done for both new employees as well as veterans.

BUSINESS CLASSIFICATION OF DIVERSIFIED ORGANIZATIONS

When an organization uses diversification as a tool for growth, it tends to end up with a portfolio of multiple businesses. This requires the organization to ensure that it manages this portfolio not only for sustenance, but also for furthering growth.[6]

This division of businesses in a diversified organization is done based on two dimensions: (the BCG Matrix) relative market share of the business in a particular industry, and the relative growth rate of the industry. It is assumed that higher market share also leads to greater profitability for the organization. Every business that a diversified organization possesses can be put in one of the four quadrants in the two-dimensional matrix.

There may be businesses that enjoy high market share (with correspondingly high cash generation), but at the same time are not growing quickly (with correspondingly low spending). Such businesses are labelled as 'cash cows': sources of cash for other divisions of the diversified organization.

The second category of businesses fall in the category of 'dogs'. These divisions operate with a low growth rate, and at the same time generate low to modest cash flows. A dog's surplus cash flow is generally required to be reinvested in the same business.

The third category of businesses are characterized by a high growth rate but low market share. Heavy investment is required to maintain this market share, and even more is needed for the market share to increase. These 'question marks' often eat up a lot of organizational resources, in the hope that some day they will gain higher market share and become more profitable.

The fourth category of businesses is what any diversified organization aspires to possess. The 'stars' are the businesses which not only enjoy high market share but also a high growth rate.

These businesses need not be financially self-reliant at this stage, but small inputs of cash often make them high generators of cash in the future. The success mantra lies in transforming the businesses titled as question marks into stars and then these into cash cows. A blunder sequence would be the change in status of a business from a cash cow to a dog, or a star to a question mark to a dog.

ILLUSTRATIONS

Illustration I: The Tata Group

Having reached the pinnacle of being the wealthiest business house in India,[7] let us understand the diversification journey through the Tata Group. The Tata Group[8] was founded by Jamshedji Tata as a trading company in 1868—the foundation for the Tata Group of today. In 1874, he ventured into textiles, and by 1904, had the luxurious Taj Hotel under the group's umbrella. That same year, Dorab Tata, eldest son of Jamshedji, took over as chairman of the organization. The group, under his leadership, had diversified into steel by 1912. Subsequent diversification moves were into hydroelectric power, cooking oil, and cement. Dorab was also instrumental in the founding of the Indian Institute of Sciences, Bangalore. The next chairman of the group, J.R.D. Tata, brought aviation services into the group's portfolio. Unfortunately, in 1953 the airline business was nationalized post-Independence. Many other domains were explored, such as chemicals, information technology, automobiles, tea, etc. In 1991, the group came under the leadership of Ratan Tata. He was instrumental in taking the Tata brand into the global arena, be it based on organic or inorganic growth. Most of the inorganic channels of diversification were acquisitions of foreign players, such as the Tetley Group

(UK), Daewoo (South Korea), Corus (UK), and Jaguar and Land Rover (UK).

The Tata Group is a live example of how a diversified organization succeeded in an emerging economy. Since the group was aware that the available talent pool was limited, it instituted Tata Administrative Services (TAS) for growing fresh talent into leadership roles in different businesses. By rotating them across businesses and across the group's functions, they became competent enough to tackle the nuances of the group's various ventures. Given the credibility of the group, bankers aren't reluctant to fund their projects. Also, if we look at the Tata Group's businesses, we see that many ventures are quite unrelated to each other. We discussed earlier how such conglomerates have higher success in emerging markets, and needless to say, if the group is the wealthiest in India, it definitely can be labelled as immensely successful.

This illustration also brings to the fore the different categories of the Tata Group's businesses. Tata Motors, Tata Teleservices, Tata Tea, Tata Steel, Voltas, TCS, Taj Hotels and Palaces, etc., can all be classified as either cash cows, dogs, question marks, or stars. This shows how a well-diversified organization is positioned in different quadrants of the BCG matrix. A temporal analysis of any of the businesses will help us understand the way in which a venture moves from one quadrant to another. For example, we may say that Tata Motors has moved from being a question mark to a star.

Illustration II: Microsoft

The growth trajectory of Microsoft is quite different from that of the Tata Group. Microsoft is a relatively young organization, established in 1975 by Bill Gates.[9] Founding partner Paul Allen later dropped out due to health issues. The organization started off with only one product, the BASIC, with an intent to sell this programming language for personal computer users. The company's first break came when a deal was struck with IBM, in which Microsoft was entrusted with the task of providing the operating system for its personal computers. This required Microsoft to acquire an organization with a product that was renamed to what we popularly know as MS-DOS. Windows OS was introduced in the 1980s, followed by Windows NT. Microsoft Network (MSN) was introduced in 1995, on the cusp of the internet revolution.

Windows Vista was launched in 2006. The company's foray into Vista was a landmark, because Windows, Microsoft's flagship product, had such complex codes that the organization was finding it difficult to come up with upgrades fast. Vista was developed by making the codes simple enough for the organization to react with agility in case of a better offering from a competitor. Movement into MSN was equally sweeping—after all, the organization moved into the unexplored domains of web searches, electronic mailing, chats, instant messaging, etc. Some of these movements were based on acquisitions, while others were done in-house. The organization decided to enter the enterprise software market, again by acquisition, but with a focus on small and medium enterprises. This was done deliberately to ensure that it did not come head on with giants in the ERP industry like SAP and Oracle. Such moves offer a classic case of how Microsoft used diversification as a strategic tool for growth.

Illustration III: Videocon

Videocon has traditionally been present in the domains of home appliances, such as ovens, refrigerators, washing machines, and air conditioners. Over time, it has also moved into consumer electronics such as televisions and audio/video devices.[10] Diversification was the need of the hour for this organization, given that the majority of its businesses are located in the emerging market of India. The organization also ventured into shipping and trading by acquiring the Shipping Corporation of India and State Trading Corporation. Subsequently, the movement into oil exploration has been profitable. However, all of Videocon's moves were not financially rewarding. For example, diversification into real estate and financial services proved to be detrimental to the organization's financial health. Videocon is looking at entertainment as the next big thing to be added to its already diversified portfolio. As of now, the organization considers its consumer durables businesses and its oil ventures as its stars[11].

CONCLUSION

The definition of diversification has undergone a change in light of new developments. It is not only a presence in multiple businesses, but also the relative profit contribution of each business in the overall organizational kitty. The nature of diversification can range from 'single business' to 'unrelated', and the location of the organization in this spectrum is based on conditions that we discussed in the first section ('Understanding Diversification'). Diversification as a strategic tool for growth is very resource intensive, and an organization should perform an in-depth analysis prior to taking up such a business move ('Checklist for Success through Diversification'). The benefits of going this route have been more successful in emerging markets ('Benefits of Diversification in Emerging Markets'), but the benefits are conditioned not by only external factors such as emerging/

developed markets, but also on internal factors such as the way in which portfolios are maintained ('Business Classification of Diversified Organizations').

NOTES

1. Salter, M.S. and Porter, M.E. (1986). 'Note on Diversification as a Strategy', *Harvard Business School Note.*

2. Rumelt, R.P. (1982). 'Diversification Strategy and Profitability', *Strategic Management Journal*, 3(4), pp. 359–70.

3. Markides, C.C. (1997). 'To Diversify or not to Diversify', *Harvard Business Review.*

4. Barney, J. (1986). 'Strategic Factor Markets: Expectations, Luck, and Business Strategy', *Management Science*, 32 (10), pp. 1231–41; Barney, J.B. (1991). 'Firm Resources and Sustained Competitive Advantage', *Journal of Management*, 17 (1), pp. 99–120.

5. Khanna, T. and Palepu, K. (1997). 'Why Focused Strategies May be Wrong for Emerging Markets?', *Harvard Business Review*, 75 (4), pp. 41–51.

6. Allan, G.B. (1975). 'A note on BCG concept of competitive analysis and corporate strategy', President and Fellows of Harvard College.

7. Excerpted from http://www.ibtimes.com/articles/43589/20100816/tata-reliance-industries-ratan-tata-sterlite-bharti-airtel-mukesh-ambani-anil-ambani.htm on 25 September 2010.

8. Excerpted from http://www.scribd.com/doc/29773455/Journey-of-TATA on 16 August 2010.

9. Excerpted from http://www.microsoft.com/presspass/insidems.mspx on 17 August 2010.

10. Excerpted from www.videoconworld.com on 17 August 2010.

11. Excerpted from http://www.financialexpress.com/news/videocon-tuning-into-the-big-picture/74407/0 on 17 August 2010.

7

Growth through Strategic Alliances

INTRODUCTION

Organizations have realized that it is not always judicious to foray into every area of interest. The organization may lack some required capabilities or the resources. Sometimes building those capabilities is better done in an existing business. In such situations, it is always advisable that the organization partners with another organization which is equally keen, but one that lacks certain capabilities as well. Such a phenomenon wherein both the organizations pool in their resources is what we call strategic alliancing. Such partnerships have fuelled growth for a large number of organizations, more so in recent times.

UNDERSTANDING STRATEGIC ALLIANCES— THE KEY CONCEPT

A strategic alliance is where two organizations come together to fulfil a specific business objective. At the operational level, such an objective may take any form, but at the strategic level, the key objective is often growth. The alliance may be registered as a separate legal entity, or may be a make-shift arrangement. At times, the strategic alliance becomes an organization on its own. There are different types of arrangement between organizations, but all do not qualify to be considered as strategic alliances (see Figure 7.1).[1]

As the figure shows, relationships between organizations can be either contractual or equity arrangements. Contractual arrangements are the ones in which the organizations are bound to deliver the commitment based on a legal (or even implicit) tie-up. On the other hand, equity arrangements are such that there is shared ownership of the venture, making it mutually beneficial. There is a direct gain herein—profits are directly shared by organizations entering the equity arrangement, based on the ratio in which the equity is held. As we see from the shaded area, the organizational arrangement should be a 'less than arm's-length relationship'[2] for it to be a strategic alliance.

STRATEGIC ALLIANCE TYPES AND ULTIMATE OUTCOME

Studies have shown that the final destiny of an alliance is contingent upon its type. Here, the typology of strategic alliances is defined by the stature of the organizations involved. Accordingly, there are six types of strategic alliances[3], and each type is expected to follow a particular path.

The first type is one in which *direct competitors join hands*. The organizations have similar products targeted to almost the same customer segments in the same geographies. As a result, it is felt *ex ante* that by collaborating, great synergy will be achieved. Indeed, there is an increase in business since the cost of showing one organization to be better than the competitor is no longer

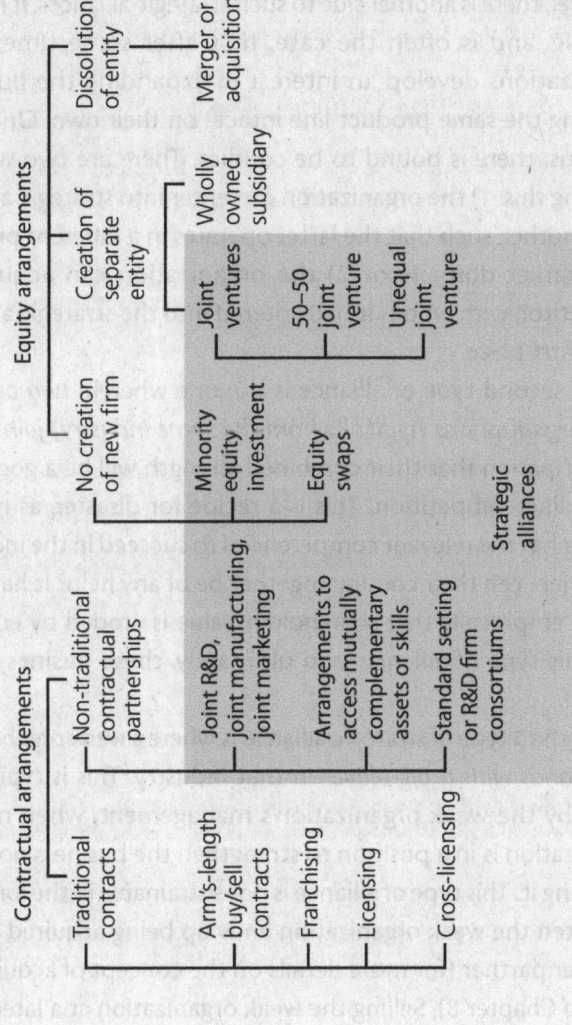

FIGURE 7.1: GROWTH THROUGH STRATEGIC ALLIANCES

Scope of interfirm relationships

Contractual arrangements
- Traditional contracts
  - Arm's-length buy/sell contracts
  - Franchising
  - Licensing
  - Cross-licensing
- Non-traditional contractual partnerships
  - Joint R&D, joint manufacturing, joint marketing
  - Arrangements to access complementary assets or skills
  - Standard setting or R&D firm consortiums

Equity arrangements
- No creation of new firm
  - Minority equity investment
  - Equity swaps
- Creation of separate entity
  - Joint ventures
    - 50–50 joint venture
    - Unequal joint venture
  - Wholly owned subsidiary

Dissolution of entity
- Merger or acquisition

Strategic alliances

Source: Adapted from Yoshino and Rangan, 1995, as cited in Kale and Singh, 2009.

required. Also, there is a feeling, at least during the relationship's inception, that neither organization is relinquishing command. However, there is another side to such strategic alliances. It is quite possible, and is often the case, that after some time, both organizations develop an interest in expanding the business (keeping the same product line intact) on their own. Once this happens, there is bound to be conflict. There are two ways of avoiding this: 1) the organization can enter into strategic alliance with another, such that the latter operates in a different product and market domain, or 2) the organization can acquire its competitor, with whom it had entered into the strategic alliance in the first place.

The second type of alliance is the one wherein *two or more weak organizations (typically from the same industry) join hands* in anticipation that their combined strength will be a good way of tackling competition. This is a recipe for disaster, as neither partner has the relevant competencies to succeed in the industry. How then, can their coming together be of any help? It has been shown empirically that shareholder value is eroded by entering into this type of alliance, and ultimately, these businesses are sold off.

The third type of strategic alliance is where a *weak organization joins hands with a big player* in that industry. This is typically a move by the weak organization's management, when neither organization is in a position to strengthen the business nor keen on selling it. This type of alliance is not sustainable in the long run, and often the weak organization ends up being acquired by the stronger partner (for more details on the concept of acquisition, refer to Chapter 8). Selling the weak organization at a later stage reduces its bargaining power, leading to loss of shareholder value in the acquisition. So, if an organization understands that it is too weak to sustain in an industry, it should ideally partner with an organization which is potentially an ideal buyer at a later stage. The typical profile of the ideal buyer is an organization which is a strong player in that industry, and has sufficient financial back-up to later acquire the weaker organization. There is a word of caution that we should raise here—the weak organization should only make such a move if it is sure that the business in question can be separated from other businesses without any loss of overall capability.

The fourth type of strategic alliance is the one in which a *weak organization enters into an arrangement with a strong organization of the same industry*, with the *sole aim of learning the success mantra from the latter*. The weak organization's objective is to grow strong and then exit the alliance for subsequent stand-alone operations. To succeed, its focus should be on key functions and expertise. These arrangements, also known as bootstrap alliances, are very difficult to execute with the learning objective in mind. In most cases, the weak organization is not able to gain much, and is finally acquired by the alliance partner.

In the penultimate type of alliances, we see *two organizations of similar high strength (also compatible)* coming together. In the initial phase of the strategic alliance, it is felt that both organizations share similar bargaining power, but as time progresses, one partner becomes more powerful than the other, thereby increasing its bargaining power and leading to the sale of the other organization. This shift in relative power can be a result of internal or external factors. An important external factor is industry dynamics; if the industry is moving in a direction wherein the assets of one organization become more important in delivering value to customers, then that organization is bound to become stronger in the alliance.

The most successful type of alliance is the one in which *organizations of similar stature but with distinctly complementary capabilities* forge a partnership. These strategic alliances tend to last, and there is low tendency of shift in bargaining power. The alliance partners offer different value propositions to different markets altogether. The challenge here is operations. Since both the organizations have quite different businesses, their management patterns and ethical norms are also bound to differ. Arriving at a convergence on how the alliance will be managed will determine whether the partnership is successful or not.

CRITICAL SUCCESS FACTORS IN DIFFERENT ALLIANCE STAGES

The above section dealt with the different types of alliances. We also need to understand that there is no sweeping heuristic to be followed for a strategic alliance to succeed. The alliance, as an entity, passes through different stages of life, each unique in nature, along with the factors that decide whether the alliance will be able to address the challenges of that stage and pass to the next or not. The different stages and the respective critical factors[4] that decide on the success are depicted in Figure 7.2.

The above portrait divides the alliance's life cycle into three stages: the beginning of partner selection and alliance formation, formation of norms and structure, and management. This section discusses the factors that determine the success of strategic alliances based on the three stages.

Stage I: Pre-formation of the Alliance

Once an organization has decided that it can meet a specific business objective by entering into a strategic alliance, the natural challenge is to evaluate the potential partner. It is not only the

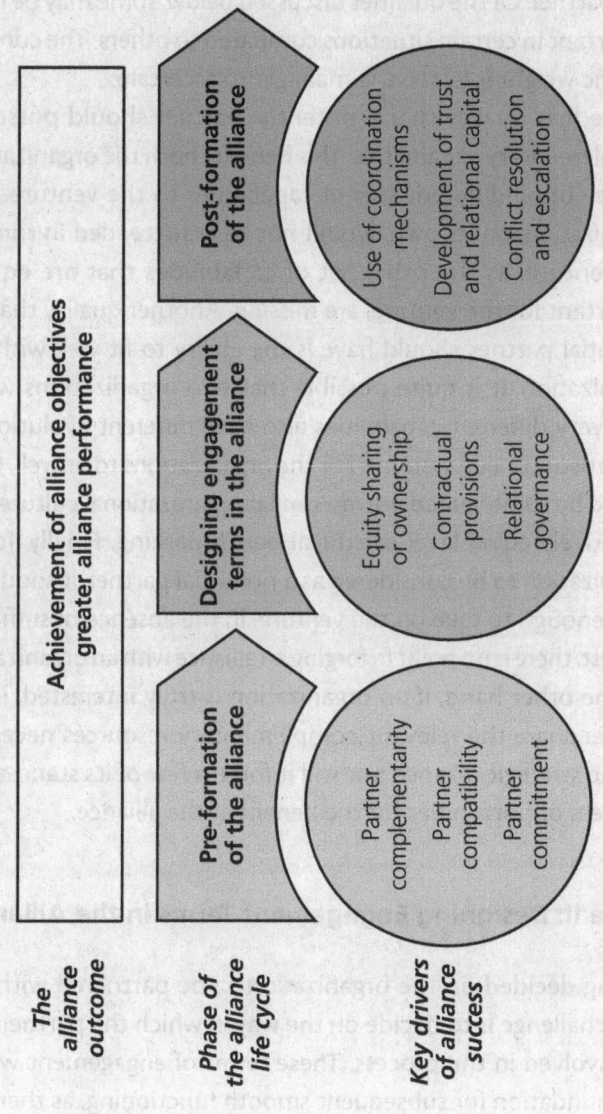

FIGURE 7.2: ASSESSMENT OF ACHIEVEMENT OF ALLIANCE OBJECTIVE

The alliance outcome

Achievement of alliance objectives greater alliance performance

Phase of the alliance life cycle

Pre-formation of the alliance

Designing engagement terms in the alliance

Post-formation of the alliance

Key drivers of alliance success

Partner complementarity

Partner compatibility

Partner commitment

Equity sharing or ownership

Contractual provisions

Relational governance

Use of coordination mechanisms

Development of trust and relational capital

Conflict resolution and escalation

Source: Adapted from Kale and Singh, 2009.

partner's qualities that matter, but their ability to gel with their new partner. Of the qualities discussed below, some may be more important in certain situations compared to others. The context-specific weight is left to the manager to ascertain.

The first quality that a potential partner should possess is complementary capabilities. This benefits both the organizations as they bring different sets of capabilities to the venture. One organization, on its own, would not have succeeded in running the venture, as the other set of capabilities that are equally important for the venture, are missing. Another quality that the potential partner should have is the ability to fit well with this organization. It is quite possible that two organizations which have very different capabilities also have different evolutionary patterns and value systems. For the organizations to fit well, there should be some shared norms, similar organizational culture, and a relatively equal level of ethical benchmarking. Finally, for an organization to be considered as a potential partner, it should be keen enough to take on the venture. In the absence of sufficient interest, there is no point in forging an alliance with an organization. On the other hand, if an organization is truly interested, it will neither share the relevant complementary resources necessary for the strategic alliance nor will it forgo a few of its stand-alone business opportunities for the benefit of the alliance.

Stage II: Designing Engagement Terms in the Alliance

Having decided on the organization to be partnered with, the next challenge is to decide on the way in which the partners will get involved in the process. These terms of engagement will be the foundation for subsequent smooth functioning, as there is a tendency for opportunistic behaviour by one of the partners after the strategic alliance has been entered into. This can be detrimental to the overall functioning of the alliance, and the objective with which the alliance had been formed may be defeated altogether. However, if both partner organizations have equal interest in the success of the venture and benefit from it, then the chances of opportunistic behaviour are minimized. A tool to achieve this is by ensuring that both partners have equity ownership. There is another benefit that equity participation ensures—the proportion of equity holding determines the level of profit sharing. In the absence of such clear-cut sharing mechanisms, there are chances of heartburn. For example, one organization may contest that its contribution in the strategic alliance is more than the proportion of profit that it has been entitled to, in the contract that was decided *a priori*. However, if there is equity participation, then the equity ratio itself decides the contribution of each organization. There are other factors that decide the robustness of engagement terms as well. As far as possible, the mutual obligations and rights of both the partners should be spelled out clearly by way of contracts. Needless to say, no business relation of this nature can exist if the organizations don't share trust and goodwill.

Stage III: Post-formation of the Alliance

This is the stage where the strategic alliance is actually functional. It is time for the organizations, after being diligent enough to choose the right partner and set the right terms of engagement, to reap the expected benefits with which the alliance was formed in the first place. However, this is possible only if the alliance is functioning in the desired fashion.

At the functional level, smooth operations depend largely on the way the organizations orchestrate their activities, specific to the alliance. Both partners are expected to perform certain activities in a coordinated way. To achieve this, the activities and deliverables of both the organizations should be spelt out, along with each activity's timeline. Mutual trust between partners is equally essential. This reduces friction, and the cost associated with developing elaborate monitoring mechanisms is also minimal. There is another benefit that the alliance derives out of the mutual trust between partner organizations. Post-alliance formation, many unforeseen issues can crop up—if there is trust between the partners, then firefighting is easier.

BENEFITS OF A DEDICATED ALLIANCE FUNCTION

We discussed earlier the different stages of a strategic alliance (that is, the life cycle), and also the checklist of things that each partner organization should ensure for the success of the alliance. To carry out the entire checklist, it would be unwise for an organization to dedicate all resources available to it. There needs to be a function which accounts for all the expertise an organization requires to manage all stages of a strategic alliance[5]. Let such a dedicated department be labelled as the alliance function. The benefits of such a function are captured in Figure 7.3. Benefits have been elaborated below.

Management of Learning and Knowledge

A dedicated alliance function acts as a reservoir where accumulation of knowledge from previous alliances takes place. Once an organization decides to enter into a strategic alliance, there are certain stage-specific life-cycle capabilities that determine success (refer to the section, 'Critical Success Factors'). By seeking feedback

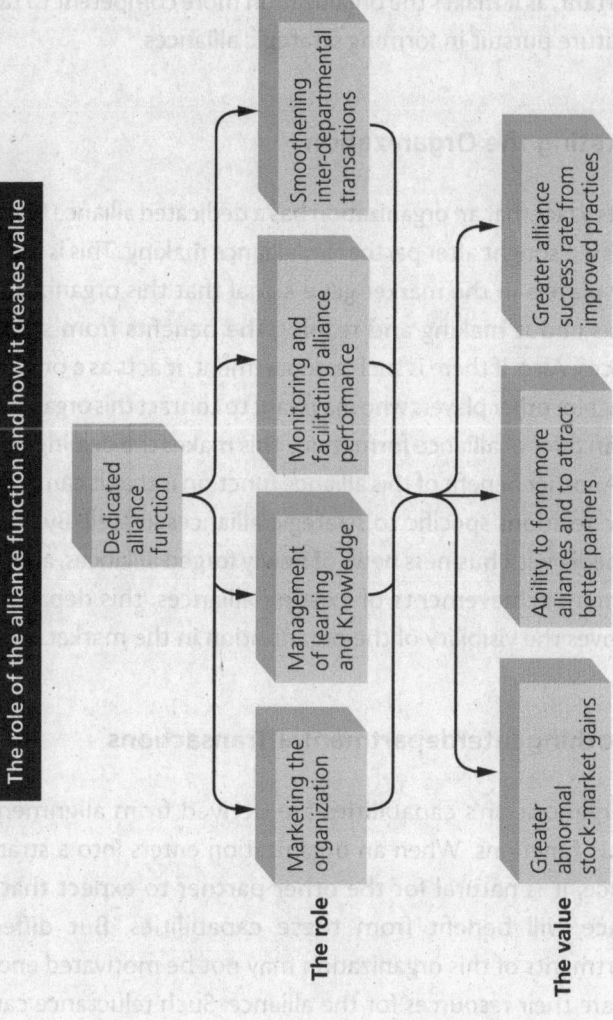

FIGURE 7.3

The role of the alliance function and how it creates value

The role

Dedicated alliance function

- Marketing the organization
- Management of learning and Knowledge
- Monitoring and facilitating alliance performance
- Smoothening inter-departmental transactions

The value

- Greater abnormal stock-market gains
- Ability to form more alliances and to attract better partners
- Greater alliance success rate from improved practices

Source: Adapted from Dyer, Kale, and Singh, 2001.

from current ventures, such a department also imbibes learning from ongoing partnerships. This repository of knowledge is important, as it makes the organization more competent to tackle any future pursuit in forming strategic alliances.

Marketing the Organization

The very fact that an organization has a dedicated alliance function makes it a sought after partner for alliance making. This is because other players in the market get a signal that this organization is serious about making and reaping the benefits from strategic alliances. Also, if there is such a department, it acts as a one-point contact for other players who may want to contact this organization with an offer of alliance formation. This makes the dealing hassle-free. Another benefit of this alliance function is that it can manage public relations specific to strategic alliances as well. By feeding the media with business news of newly forged alliances, as well as landmark achievements of existing alliances, this department improves the visibility of the organization in the market.

Smoothing Interdepartmental Transactions

An organization's capabilities are derived from alignment of various functions. When an organization enters into a strategic alliance, it is natural for the other partner to expect that the alliance will benefit from these capabilities. But different departments of this organization may not be motivated enough to share their resources for the alliance. Such reluctance can be nullified if there is a dedicated function (specializing in alliances) explicitly seeking the exact nature of resources from respective departments. This dedicated function will then also ensure that respective departments work in sync with each other for the overall benefit of the alliance.

Monitoring and Facilitating Alliance Performance

A dedicated alliance department ensures that the strategic alliance is performing as per the expected benchmarks. In case any support is sought, this department can intervene and draw resources from organizational functions. This department may also evaluate the benchmarks of expected performance, and revisit them time and again in light of new developments.

ILLUSTRATIONS

Illustration I: Bharti Airtel's Partnership with Ericsson

Bharti Airtel Limited is an integrated telecom service provider with operations spread across nineteen countries in Asia and Africa. The businesses of the organization comprise four strategic business units (SBUs)—Mobile, Telemedia, Enterprise, and Digital TV. Of these, the Mobile SBU offers services in India, Bangladesh, and Sri Lanka. In India, Airtel is the telecom service provider that enjoys the largest number of customers, spread across twenty-three telecom circles.[6]

Ericsson, founded in 1876 in Sweden, on the other hand, is a hardware-based organization, and specializes in providing technology and services to telecom operators. The business portfolio ranges from telecom (mobile and fixed network) infrastructure, telecom services, broadband and multimedia solution for operators, etc.

Bharti Airtel and Ericsson have been collaborating for quite some time. In March 2010, they entered into a partnership for network expansion.[7] To us, such an alliance makes huge sense. Both organizations have complementary capabilities—Airtel being number one in the business of telecom services, and Ericsson's forte being provision of telecom network infrastructure management. Also, the organizations operate on similar scales in their respective markets. We discussed in 'Strategic Alliance Types and Ultimate Outcomes' that such alliances have highest probability of long-term success.

Illustration II: The M-Budget Credit Card

This illustration speaks of a strategic alliance forged between GE Money Bank, Migros, and MasterCard. Before giving details, it is better that we develop a brief understanding of the three organizations.

GE Money Bank was established about thirty-five years ago, and is in the business of providing finance to individuals for cars and other vehicles: insurance, credit cards, and savings accounts. It entered Switzerland by acquiring two banks in 1997, and then brought these two entities under its umbrella brand of GE Money Bank.[8] Migros, on the other hand, is a Switzerland-based retail organization founded in 1925. In the country, it operates at a scale which makes it the largest chain of supermarkets, as well as the biggest employer. M-budget is an initiative of Migros, wherein a portfolio of around 300+ products is offered in the supermarket, specifically targeted to customers with low incomes and big families.

In 2006, GE Money Bank and Migros entered into a strategic alliance to offer a new product, the M-Budget credit card. Initially, it had annual fees, though much lower than other cards. This fee was scrapped, due to a specific movement in the market. Based on the heuristics that we discussed earlier, this strategic alliance also made sense. Both the organizations were big players in their respective domains and were into businesses which did not overlap. The products and markets were complementary, and a strategic alliance was a good way of integrating the strengths of both these organizations for mutual benefit. GE Money Bank had expertise in financial products, so designing the credit card offering wasn't a big task for it. At the same time, Migros had the expertise in the vast distribution of products, to customers at all strata of society. The credit card, channelled through the network of superstores, was a good way of reaching out to a wide audience.

Illustration III: ICICI-Prudential Life Insurance Company

ICICI-Prudential Life Insurance is an equity joint venture between ICICI Bank (India) and Prudential Plc (UK). In this alliance, ICICI Bank has an equity participation of 74 percent and Prudential, 26 percent. Both organizations operate in the domain of financial services, though in different markets. The joint venture was conceived in 2000, and is today one of the largest life insurers in India. In an annual survey conducted by the *Economic Times*–AC Nielsen ORG Marg, the joint venture has been rated the most trusted private life insurer three years in a row.[9]

There is a reason for this. Both organizations have a strong understanding of the financial services industry. Having come together for a venture, again in financial services (life insurance), gives them the natural benefit of previous domain knowledge. However, there could be a future challenge for the joint venture. Both organizations are in financial services, and the only complementarity that they enjoy is in markets in which they operate. Both may have an interest in rolling out stand-alone insurance operations in India once they have learned the nuances of the business—nuances of life insurance for ICICI and nuances of the Indian market for Prudential, Plc. Only time will tell how valid this concern may be.

CONCLUSION

Strategic alliances are partnerships between two or more organizations, which come together to fulfil a common business objective ('Understanding Strategic Alliances'). As discussed earlier, these partnerships may take the form of either contractual or equity arrangements between organizations. It is the type of organizations that enter into strategic alliances that determine whether the venture will succeed or not. It has been found that when organizations with distinctly complementary capabilities come together, the chances of success are the highest ('Strategic Alliances Types and Ultimate Outcomes'). Different stages of a strategic alliance dictate different requirements from partner organizations, and the management of these requirements determines the venture's success ('Critical Success Factors in Different Alliance Stages'). Management of the alliance becomes easier if the organizations have a function dedicated to the formation/running of the strategic alliance ('Benefits of a Dedicated Alliance Function').

NOTES

1. Yoshino, M.Y. and Srinivasa, R.U. (1995). *Strategic Alliances: An Entrepreneurial Approach to Globalization*. Boston: Harvard Business

School Press as cited in Kale, P. and Singh, H. (2009). 'Managing Strategic Alliances: What do we know, and where do we go from here?' *Academy of Management Perspectives*, 23(3), pp. 45–62.

2. Davies, W. (2004). *The Art of Strategic Management: Strategic Alliances* (vol 2). Mumbai: Jaico Publishing House.

3. Bleeke, J. and Ernst, D. (1995). 'Is your strategic alliance really a sale?' *Harvard Business Review*, 73 (1), pp. 97–105.

4. Kale, P. and Singh, H. (2009), pp. 45–62.

5. Dyer, J.H., Kale, P. and Singh, H. (2001). 'How to make strategic alliances work', *MIT Sloan Management Review*, 42 (4), pp. 37–43.

6. Excerpted from http://www.airtel.in/wps/wcm/connect/about+bharti+ airtel/Bharti+Airtel/About+Bharti+Airtel/?WCM_Page.ResetAll=TRUE&CACHE=NONE&CONTENTCACHE=NONE&CONNECTORCACHE=NONE&SRV=Page on 19 August 2010.

7. Excerpted from http://www.airtel.in/wps/wcm/connect/About%20 Bharti%20Airtel/bharti+airtel/media+centre/bharti+airtel+news/ mobile/pg-bharti-airtel-extends-partnership-with-ericsson on 19 August 2010.

8. Excerpted from http://www.gemoneybank.ch/en/ueber_uns/ueber_ ge_money_bank/facts_und_figures.html on 19 August 2010.

9. Excerpted from http://www.iciciprulife.com/public/About-us/ About-Us.htm on 19 August 2010.

8

Growth through Mergers and Acquisitions

INTRODUCTION

Mergers and acquisitions (M&As) are inorganic tools of growth for an organization. We see, at times, that M&A is the most sought after growth tool, given the speed at which growth is achieved by the organization once an M&A deal is successfully executed. However, M&As often fail. This is because there is a fine art associated with the way mergers or acquisitions should be dealt with. This process is fraught with challenges, and an organization should have the capability to execute the deal with great diligence to ensure success—after all, an M&A is often done with the end objective of growth.

KEY CONCEPTS

Mergers and Acquisitions

We often find that the terms merger and acquisition are used interchangeably. Hence, it would be apt for us to give a clear understanding of these two growth channels. Put simply, a merger is a phenomenon where two organizations of relatively equal size decide to come together to form a single new organization. The owners of both pre-merged organizations become owners of this new entity, in a pre-decided equity format. The pre-merged organizations cease to exist once the merger is done. The equity of the two organizations is surrendered, and fresh equity of the newly formed organization, as a result of the merger, is issued to the equity holders. Though not necessary, it is often seen that mergers take place between organizations of similar stature. There seems to be some dispute on this understanding of the concept of merger, as some authors[1] prefer to call this phenomenon 'consolidation.' Their definition of a merger is similar to how we have understood the idea of acquisition, as detailed in the following section.

In case the pre-merged organizations are competitors, then the merger is termed as horizontal. A horizontal merger leads to greater market share in a specific industry for the merged entity. While merging horizontally, the organizations need to be cautious about the anti-monopoly laws of the land. This is because, as the merger leads to increase in market power of the new entity, it inherently may come under the scanner of the anti-monopoly regulator. Along similar lines, when two organizations that share a seller–buyer relationship merge, then the phenomenon is labelled as a vertical merger. A vertical merger increases the control (and related bargaining power) of the merged entity over the value chain, over and above ensuring that the merged entity captures the profits it had to previously forgo in the buyer–seller transactions. On the flip side, such a merger ensures that there is deeper engagement of the merged organization in the industry. In the eventuality of the industry becoming unattractive, a vertical merger may make the exit of the merged entity difficult from the industry. Apart from horizontal and vertical mergers, there is a third type of merger, the conglomerate merger. In a conglomerate merger, two organizations with presence in different and unrelated industries come together. Growth through conglomerate mergers has proven to be immensely useful in emerging economies.[2]

Acquisition, on the other hand, is the phenomenon where one organization takes over the ownership of another. The organization that has been taken over is often referred to as the 'target' in M&A parlance. After being acquired, the target organization ceases to exist. The equity holders of the target are given shares of the acquiring organization, based on an exchange formula, also known as the swap ratio.

Friendly Acquisition versus Hostile Takeover

As we saw earlier, acquisition involves one organization being taken over by another. This may happen either with or without the consent of the management of the target organization. If the acquiring organization takes over the target with the prior consent of its board (that is, the management), then the acquisition is said to be friendly in nature. However, there are instances where the board of the prospective target refuses the deal. In such situations, if the acquiring organization still decides to go ahead with the acquisition by way of purchasing equity of the target from shareholders, then the takeover is termed as hostile. Hostile takeovers are often characterized by the exodus of the target's top management team, along with key personnel loyal to the top management. Often, acquisitions are affected with the objective of accessing complementary capabilities. Such capabilities generally lie in human resources; if an unfriendly takeover leads to attrition of key human resources, then the very purpose of the acquisition is defeated. In light of this, acquiring organizations should have an a priori understanding of the benefits sought from the acquisition–if the move is to acquire complementary tacit resources, then the organization would do better by deciding to take the route of friendly acquisition. Given the benefits that friendly acquisitions have for the acquirer, we discuss below the checklist one needs to follow for executing such a deal.

Friendly Acquisitions—The Mantra

The ability to manage an acquisition deal, such that the very purpose of the deal is achieved, is a rare one. Often, as discussed earlier, organizations fail to reap the benefits of an acquisition, because of procedural lapses. This section is dedicated to help the reader understand the checks and controls that need to be in place, in each step of the acquisition deal, to ensure success. All these steps[3] have been referred to as gates, since a successful deal needs to pass through the qualifying criteria of each gate.

Gate I: Keeping the Radar Vigilant

The possibility for acquisition can arise any time. So, it is necessary to keep the organizational radar functional at all times. This is because any miss in identifying an opportunity to acquire a strategically relevant target can lead to a loss for the organization. However, this can be a herculean task, as keeping a tab on every acquisition opportunity that comes through can be very resource intensive. Screening all potential targets, that too on a real-time basis, may be streamlined if the process of screening is disciplined.

The opportunity to acquire a target should not be reason enough to proceed with the acquisition. The deal should have an overall fit with the strategy of the acquirer. Unless the acquisition deal is aligned with the overall goals, there is no point in getting excited about the deal, irrespective of how lucrative it may seem at first. There is another reason that often leads an organization to proceed with an acquisition, even if the deal doesn't fit with the acquirer. There are times when the person (or the team) sitting at the top gets passionate about acquiring the target, without articulating any business sense. Time and again, the business environment has witnessed such deals being executed because of emotionally charged CEOs.

Gate II: Getting Priorities Straight

It is important for not only the acquirer but also the target organization to understand that it is difficult to calculate a fair value of the deal at such an early stage. Hence, all efforts should be focused on deciding if the deal makes strategic sense or not. The entire process of negotiation associated with an acquisition consumes a lot of organizational resources. Hence, a lot of planning is needed in this initial phase to understand if the merits of the potential deal are compelling enough for further investment of resources in negotiation. The acquirer organization should always keep in mind that initial perceptions of price should neither be a trigger nor an impediment in this stage. This is because the acquirer is in too early a stage to have sufficient and relevant information to arrive at a fair range of price for the target.

This gate also requires the acquirer organization to decide on some of the deal's essential attributes. These essential attributes, as expected from the target organization, should be such that they are absolutely non-negotiable from the standpoint of the acquirer. It is critical to chalk out such attributes for better understanding of the expectation of the acquirer by the target—after all, these are the ones the acquirer would like to hold as fixed. In case of a mismatch, the deal may be called off at this stage, rather than these expectations being spelled out later, making the act of pulling out expensive for the acquirer.

It is beneficial if the acquirer spells out the role and fate of the top management team of the target organization at this stage, as part of the deal's essential attributes. While doing so, the acquirer should try to be as humane as possible, at least in their approach. During such acquisition negotiations, it is natural for the management team of the target organization to undergo a lot of anxiety and suspicion. The negotiation should be channelled in such a way that the team from the prospective target feels that it is mutually beneficial to go ahead with the deal, and that their future is brighter (by way of career prospects) if the deal is struck.

Gate III: Pre-negotiation

After initial screening of the prospective target and before final negotiation with the organization for acquisition, there is an important step. In this phase of the deal, the acquirer organization conducts a thorough check of the standing of the prospective target. This helps in cross-checking the claims and perception of the target. There is another benefit of conducting this thorough check—it helps the acquirer organization to gather information on the nuances of the internal operating environment of the target. By doing so, the acquirer can develop a sense of whether the values, systems, and processes of the target are suitable enough for integration with the acquirer.

This step is better known as the stage of due diligence. During this stage, the technical team of the acquiring organization should wear the lens of investigators. From detailed scrutiny of financial records to checking legal compliance, this step is all-encompassing as far as fact finding is concerned. Unfortunately, such a holistic scrutiny of the target organization is often left to junior personnel as this is seen as repetitive and mundane. A seasoned acquirer, however, ensures that the top management team originally dealing with the target is deeply engaged in the process of due diligence.

Gate IV: Striking the Deal

This is the actual step where acquisition takes place, and the acquiring organization grows. While most of the broad terms of purchase have already been set out in previous stages, this is the stage where detailed and granular deal details are worked out. This is also the stage where differences of opinion are ironed out to the satisfaction of both parties. This being an advanced stage of the deal, the acquirer should ensure it focuses only on priority issues, or else there is a chance that trivial issues take up most of the resources, leaving little or no room for negotiation for high-priority items. Also, rather than a single team working on the deal, there should be multiple teams, drawn along functional lines, to look into the details. This way, there would be a team of lawyers from both sides working on legal aspects, and another team of finance experts working on the deal's structure. The details of how to pay for a deal is covered in the subsequent section.

While working on the deal, there are two important factors that the acquiring organization needs to factor in. On the one hand, the acquirer should not only focus on the target with which the deal is being finally negotiated, but should also simultaneously aspire to look at other alternative targets that comes its way. If such an acquisition with another target takes place midway in the negotiations with the current target, then this increases the bargaining power of the acquirer. On the other hand, the acquirer should also be aware of the fact that acquisition of the proposed target organization might face competition. Deals are more prone to such competition in the case of structured auctions; however, acquirer organizations should not let their guard down even in the case of dedicated deal negotiations with a prospective target.

Gate V: Deal Closure and Integration

Once the deal has been done, the acquirer needs to ensure two important things. One, the acquirer needs to ensure that it is able to convince all its stakeholders about the merits of the deal. Two, the acquirer needs to ensure that the acquired organization is well integrated. Both these steps mandate that the acquirer is fast and calculative in communicating the acquisition details and future plans to both the stakeholders as well as personnel of the acquired organization. The nuances of executing a smooth integration are covered in a subsequent section.

MODES OF DEAL PAYMENT

Once a deal for acquisition is struck, the shareholders of the acquired organization need to be appropriately compensated. At an elemental level, payment may take place purely in either cash or stock. In practice, many hybrid options are also available, but for the sake of simplicity, we stick to an understanding of these two modes. Each has associated pros and cons, and the mode of payment is contingent upon the situation under which the growth strategy is executed.

Cash

If a deal is paid in cash, then the shareholders of the acquired organization cede any ownership in the acquired organization. All shares of the acquired company are bought by the acquiring organization; such a deal keeps the ownership structure of the acquiring organization unaltered. Needless to say, the acquiring organization needs to have sufficient liquidity to pay the entire deal amount in cash; alternatively, the cash may be sourced partly from debt instruments. Since the ownership is not diluted, this benefits the shareholders of the acquiring organization. On the flip side, if the acquisition leads to the acquirer taking a loss, the brunt is borne by its shareholders (high-risk, high-return scenario).

Stock

A deal is struck in stock if the shareholders of the acquired organization are paid shares of the acquiring organization for surrender of the target's shares. Such payment generally takes place at some predetermined exchange ratio, better known as the swap ratio. Since this leads to new shareholders being added to the ownership of the acquiring organization, the ownership of existing shareholders is diluted. Such dilution also lowers per-share earnings. Most deals in the current paradigm prefer this mode of payment. This is because such a move spreads the risk of non-realization of expected benefits across a broader base of shareholders.

ILLUSTRATIONS

Illustration I: PepsiCo's Acquisition of Quaker Oats

PepsiCo, Inc. was founded in 1965, as a result of a merger between Pepsi-Cola and Frito-Lay. The founding fathers were Donald M. Kendall (President and CEO, Pepsi-Cola) and Herman W. Lay (CEO of Frito-Lay, Inc.). Previously, Pepsi-Cola had a successful, sixty-year history of selling carbonated soft drinks.[4]

As of 1999, the key product lines of PepsiCo included carbonated soft drinks, bottled water, fruit juice, tea- and coffee-related beverages, and potato chips. PepsiCo had recently concluded a sweeping restructuring of its business operations. Quaker Oats was present in the domains of sports beverages, snack bars, ready-to-eat cereals, and grain dishes.[5] It was widely reported at that time that PepsiCo was keen on acquiring Quaker Oats, though rumours of PepsiCo's interest in Quaker Oats had been doing the rounds since 1994. It was in December 2000 that the deal was finally given a green light by the boards of both organizations.

By the end of the last century, health drinks and snacks as a trend had started picking up. Carbonated drinks were seen as a not-so-healthy option. A closer look at the PepsiCo portfolio reveals that a substantial portion of its business depended on this category of carbonated drinks. So, it was high time that PepsiCo took steps to enter into the market of drinks, to say the least, which were not perceived to be detrimental to health. The brand Gatorade, owned by Quaker Oats, was a perfect first step in such a route. Gatorade was a health drink consumed to prevent dehydration amongst athletes. Other products of Quaker Oats were also perceived to be healthy. The acquisition of Quaker Oats seemed to give a jump in the growth of PepsiCo, more so since such inorganic moves help organizations grow at a pace which can't be matched by in-house development of products and related brands.

This deal took a long time. Such detailed negotiation underscores the importance of the phases 'Pre-Negotiation' and 'Striking the Deal'. Since a lot of time was spent in understanding the expectation of both the organizations, so 'Integration' was executed without any loss of sale/resources/goodwill of the product line of erstwhile Quaker Oats. PepsiCo was very clear that, though it was deeply interested in acquiring Quaker Oats, it was 1) not ready to overpay, and 2) it would stick to the mode of payment as stock. By ensuring that these conditions were spelt out prior to any negotiations, it successfully handled the phase of 'Getting Priorities Straight'. Again, since PepsiCo was not keen on payment through cash, we understand that PepsiCo perceived some risk in this mega-deal that it did not necessarily want to pass on to its shareholders.

Illustration II: The HP–Compaq Merger

Hewlett-Packard (HP) was founded in 1939[6], and was present in almost all of the IT-related business segments (Imaging and Printing Systems, Computing Systems, and IT Services). A landmark role in history took place in 1999, when Carly Fiorina was brought in from an outside organization as CEO of HP.[7] By 2001, HP had grown to a size where its operations were present in 120 countries. In the same year, of the three business segments along which the functional division of HP was done, over 80 percent of revenues was contributed by two divisions—Imaging and Printing and Computing Systems.

Compaq is a relatively young organization, established in 1982[8] with the primary objective of manufacturing and selling computers. The first two decades of operations were fabulous, with the organization surpassing many of the previously set industry and competitor benchmarks. It was during this period that Compaq established itself as a high quality producer of PCs. The scenario began to change in 1997, when Compaq decided to move to other, more profitable regions of the industry. For example, the organization made a few acquisitions to enter high-end computers and services. Eventually, these moves were seen as an error sufficient enough to make the organization bleed. Compaq's luck refused to turn, even after the end of that century. By 2001, the dot-com bust, as well as terrorist attacks, had an adverse effect on the computer industry as a whole, impacting Compaq as well.

It was in March 2002 that the HP-Compaq merger was announced. This is a classic case, whose study helps us in understanding the fragile nature of the process of a merger, and how such moves may fail. The merger decision at HP's end was approved by a wafer-thin majority of 51.4 percent of shareholders. Many key members of the HP board came to know of such negotiations being under way quite late in the merger process. However, it is important for the management to ensure that the board, along with other key stakeholders, are brought in at a very early stage of the merger process. Overlooking this aspect was one of the reasons for dissent.[9] Simultaneously, both organizations operated in certain incompatible segments. For example, some of HP's offerings were in the high-end segment of the market (such as Imaging and Printing and IT Services) whereas Compaq's operations were primarily restricted to the low-margin PC segment. The merger meant dilution of the brand HP.

CONCLUSION

Mergers and acquisitions as strategic concepts are often used interchangeably. However, as we saw earlier, there is a subtle difference between the two. These differences range from strategic to financial and legal impact of the organizations making such moves. If an organization decides to grow by acquiring another, it may do so either by taking due consent of the management of the target organization (friendly acquisition) or by directly approaching the shareholders for purchase of equity without the prior concurrence of the management (hostile takeover). This phenomenon often leads to the exodus of the scarce talent pool of the taken-over organization, making the target organization less attractive post-acquisition. Performing the act of friendly acquisition is a fine art ('Friendly Acquisitions—The Mantra') which should be executed by following the five-stage process. A deal's success is equally contingent on the mode of payment ('Modes of Deal Payment'). Cash is preferred when the risk of the acquisition, as perceived by the acquirer, is low. In the case of a higher perceived risk, the stock of the acquirer is generally used as the mode of payment to shareholders of the target organization. Payment by stock, of course, leads to dilution of ownership for the owners of the acquirer organization.

NOTES

1. Gaughan, P.A. (2007). *Mergers, Acquisitions, and Corporate Restructuring*. New Jersey: John Wiley and Sons.
2. Khanna, T. and Palepu, K. (1990). 'Why Focused Strategies Might be Wrong for Emerging Markets', *Harvard Business Review*, 75 (4), pp. 41–51.

3. Aiello, R.J. and Watkins, M.D. (2000). 'The fine art of friendly acquisitions', *Harvard Business Review*, November, pp. 101–7.

4. Excerpted from http://www.pepsico.com/company/our-History. html on 19 August 2010.

5. Excerpted from http://www.quakeroats.com/products. aspx on 19 August 2010.

6. Excerpted from http://www8. hp.com/us/en/hp-information/about-hp/index.html on 19 August 2010.

7. Excerpted from http://en.wikipedic.org/wiki/carly Fiorina on 19 August 2010.

8. Excerpted from http://en.wikipedia.org/wiki/compaq on 19 August 2010.

9. Excerpted from http://www.businessweek.com/technology/content/feb2005/tc20050291044.tc024.htm on 19 August 2010.

Growth through Turnaround Management

INTRODUCTION

The placement of this chapter towards the end is deliberate. By now, readers have been sensitized to traditional tools of growth used by organizations. What we discuss here is something not so conventional. This chapter throws light on the tool of 'turnaround' for organizational growth. This is used by organizations that have failed miserably in the past, to such an extent that they were facing shutdown. From such a gloomy future to a state of success is a path that turns around the entire prospects of the organization.

UNDERSTANDING TURNAROUND—
THE KEY CONCEPT

As the name suggests, turnaround is a phenomenon that leads to reversal of organizational decline. In effect, there is a total 180 degree turn from the gloomy future to a brighter one. Turnaround as a tool for organizational growth is generally used when an organization has reached a stage where it is accumulating losses to an extent that survival chances appear to be bleak. Often, these organizations are on the verge of being declared as 'sick' or 'bankrupt' (possibly leading to their shutdown), unless there is a paradigm shift in the business model and/or the way in which the organization functions.

Now, whether an organization has been turned around or not is often a subjective issue. Different managerial perspectives see it differently. After all, at which stage of organizational success can we confidently declare that the organization is out of the red and back on track, and hence, the emergence of different heuristics. For example, some managers suggest that preventing the increase of losses is a sign of turnaround. Others are of the opinion that bringing an organization from a state of loss to a position of at least breaking even signifies turnaround. Still others feel breaking even falls short of the very essence of turnaround. They suggest that it is not only arresting losses and breaking even, but consistent profits (on a year-on-year basis) that decide whether an organization qualifies for turnaround or not. We subscribe to this particular definition of the phenomenon of turnaround, and propose that an organization needs to be transformed from a stage of losses (without hope of recovery) to a scenario of consistent profits for a few years before being considered as turned around.

Prior to embarking on the journey of understanding the drivers that aid in organizational turnaround, it is important for us to understand the reasons for organizational decline in the first place. The root causes of decline can be segregated into different heads, but the primary root cause that leads to an organization falling into the red is *lack of agility*. Change is the only constant, and organizational capabilities are no exception. The business environment in which an organization is housed is always changing, and this requires an organization to constantly upgrade its resources to be able to survive in this changing world. Often, when an organization has been successful for quite a period of time, it feels that the way it does business is the only way to achieve success. It becomes complacent, and gets rigid as far as its business model is concerned. Over time, there is a tendency of other organizations to overtake, and even grab, the customers of this historically successful organization. This organization, by being complacent, fails to see the cues from the market, and by the time the decline is identified, there is little possibility of damage control using conventional wisdom. Other reasons for this lack of agility can be centralized leadership (not very receptive to alternative ideas of doing business), bureaucratic organizational structure, and/or the organizational culture.

DRIVERS OF ORGANIZATIONAL TURNAROUND

With a fair idea of the meaning of organizational turnaround, let us now discuss the different aspects that are necessary for driving an organization to turn around. Each turnaround story is unique, and depending on the context, some or all of the drivers will have to be employed for successful organizational turnaround.

Leadership or Top Management Team

The role of leadership is critical for the success of any turnaround pursuit. There are different aspects of this leadership, and one such aspect is the *composition* of the top management team. By composition we mean the mix of managers who are veterans in the system vis-à-vis the leaders who join the organization with the sole motto of turning it around. Some outsiders are required in most cases—after all, existing employees feel the cause of organizational decline is the existing leaders and hence, their credibility and acumen is under severe critical review. It is felt that the mix is a function of the organizational structure that is to be turned around. Let us take examples to understand this. If a situation is such that the entire hierarchy of an organization subscribes to the same value system and it is felt that this value system is the root cause of the decline, then it probably makes sense to bring in the entire turnaround team from outside. Only then will the top management be active change agents, resulting in dislodging the extant value system and associated decline. However, there may be other situations where bringing the entire top management team from outside wouldn't be advisable. For example, in a situation where the organization operates in an extremely complex industry, or where organizational dynamics are so complex, it is not practical for an external team to internalize the nuances of these dynamics. In such a case, a healthy mix of internal and external personnel as top management would make sense. The new members may be inducted either from related or completely different domains—both have their respective merits. If leaders are brought from related industries/domains, they may bring with them the best practices of other successful organizations in related industries, which may be directly superimposed on this ailing organization. On the other hand, experts from completely new industries/domains have the tenacity to think out of the box and bring sweeping changes in a sick organization; without these experts as top managers, such changes would be unimaginable. These new leaders can learn the nuances of the complex business from incumbent managers, judge if the new, creative ideas are feasible for the current organizational context, or to understand the extent to which altering the ideas would be required.

Another aspect is the *type of leadership* that would be apt for the said organizational turnaround. Type of leadership has a definitive impact on the behavioural outcome for the employees at large. For example, if an organization is operating with minimal resources—often the case for an organization to be considered for turnaround—then there are chances that the top management will not be able to motivate employees to put in extra effort based on material incentives. However, there are higher-order incentives that may be focused on, such as motivation and recognition. In such cases, the leadership should be transformational in nature. Such transformational leadership would then motivate employees to perform better, even without any immediate monetary benefits. Also, such a style connects the employees to the top management team and the organization as a whole, to an extent that the employees develop a sense of belongingness. This adds to overall health and develops strong loyalty in the employees—the key stakeholders for any organization. Now, let us take another situation. Consider an organization that has few resources to spare for the turnaround, and the leadership is of the opinion that employees need to act in a definite fashion, as mandated by the top management. In such a case, a transactional leadership is more suited for the success of the turnaround. Herein, employees' incentives are strongly aligned with the priorities of the top management team. This triggers behaviour amongst employees sought by the leadership. Employees will definitely not take the initiative of doing things that are not only unwelcome by the leadership, but also not being considered for incentivizaiton. Hence, the leadership is interested in employee output that is transaction specific. This transactional leadership is required for a turnaround in case the leadership feels that they need discrete output from employees such that the latter do not use any judgement while delivering those outputs.

Organizational Structure

Just like leadership, structure plays a crucial role in deciding the success of the organizational turnaround. By structure we mean a whole host of factors such as autonomy, hierarchy, and division of labour. These factors are indicative, not exhaustive, in nature. The organizational structure may or may not be bureaucratic —though this can be a sign of reliability. By reliable we mean that it will act in exactly the same way, irrespective of being exposed to a particular stimulus. There are set procedures to be followed, and these procedures are explained in such detail that it leaves little (or rather no) room for human judgement while performing the activity. Such form is good when the environment is stable and the organization is established to an extent that activities and deliverables of employees are well defined. When we are looking at turnaround, such an organizational form is fraught with problems. Turnaround is a warlike situation and exposes an organization to situations that it wouldn't face day to day. Accordingly, the majority of decisions taken during this phase are unique, such that these are hard to predict or expect, leading the organization to take decisions as and when the unique situations arise. Hence, a bureaucratic organization under a turnaround situation will be a recipe for disaster.

Organizations undergoing turnaround should be very agile. This requires the top management team to make decisions fast, and to be hard taskmasters while implementing these decisions. Their agility should be to an extent that once a decision is made about a path to be followed, it should percolate so fast in the hierarchy that there is no scope for delay or discontent. Autonomy should be centralized, such that it is the sole forte of the decision makers. Other employees should have no leeway in altering their behaviour that is not aligned with the mandates of the top leadership (that is, the turnaround agents). With the above in mind, the new organizational structure should be prepared for a successful turnaround.

Financial and Operational Controls

There exists a paradox when we speak of the role of financial and operational controls, with respect to their role in the success of an organizational turnaround. On the one hand, there needs to be sufficient controls in place. After all, resources are scarce in a sick organization. This requires the entire organization to expend resources as cautiously as possible. Also, as far as possible, there should be maximum utility derived from the minimum use of available resources. However, not all employees can be entrusted to ration resources as much as possible. This brings in the role of controls like checks and balances at every stage to ensure all requisitions for resources that are not sufficiently justified are declined. There needs to be an approval matrix for access to even bare resources—this sends a strong signal to employees that they need to manage their production with the least amount of resources possible.

On the other hand, too much control for too long without exception can be detrimental to the turnaround process. After all, turning an organization around requires an innovative approach; it has been argued at multiple forums that strict controls have a tendency to impede the innovative thinking of employees. Hence, there should be phases, or instances, when these controls will have to be shed for the greater good. As said earlier, these two aspects of controls are paradoxical, where on the one hand, enforcement of stringent controls contributes to success in a turnaround, and on the other hand, the same enforcement is a bottleneck for success. Hence, an organizational turnaround should be handled with sufficient expertise to ensure selective use of these controls in the stages when they may be detrimental to the process.

Restructuring

Restructuring of the organization is generally done in all turnaround endeavours by changing the roles and responsibilities (often drastically) of employees at large, and often of the business portfolios. However, the key feature of restructuring is the mass retrenchment of employees. This is a painful process that often leads to discontent. There are employees who have been with an organization for decades, maybe even from the organization's founding. But their presence in the current state of the organization doesn't make sense any more. Under such circumstances, it would make more sense for the organization to seek their exit.

Handling such mass retrenchment often tests the skills of the best of human resources experts. There are multiple aspects that need to be taken into consideration while executing such an exercise. First of all, a message needs to be communicated that if such a retrenchment is not implemented, then organizational demise is certain and the latter would only lead to unemployment of the entire staff. It is better that a few employees are shown the door. Another aspect that needs to be considered is that only those employees whose current skills are no longer required by the organization should be retrenched. If there are employees who have skills (or the skill to learn relevant skills) that are of use to the organization, then efforts should be made to retain them (unless there are other, overriding reasons for their exit). The third aspect of retrenchment is a cultural one. If there are employees resistant to the changes proposed by the turnaround leaders, then there is no reason for them to be allowed to exist in the organization, even if they have usable skills. After all, it is the outlook of employees that makes a huge difference in the extent of a turnaround's success. Needless to say, this retrenchment should be done in such a way that other valuable employees do not feel threatened. The management needs to be humane, otherwise these valuable employees will feel discontented and the outcome can be mass outrage or even mass resignation.

Indeed, retrenchment is a key and delicate element of restructuring. However, there are other elements as well. For example, redefining the roles and responsibilities of employees is an essential ingredient. For a declining organization, it is clear that the current way of doing business won't stand. With changes in the way in which business is done, there is an automatic change in the expected contribution of its employees. This requires employees to deliver their work differently, if not deliver different work altogether. The reporting structure also changes, and employees who are otherwise used to managing an entire team may be shifted to executioners' positions. As we see, restructuring leads to a lot of changes (at all levels), and discontent is natural. The way this discontent is managed decides the success of this driver of turnaround management.

ILLUSTRATIONS

Illustration I: Scooters India Limited

Scooters India Limited was founded in 1972 as a result of assets purchased from an Italian organization, Innocenti.[1] These assets included not only plants and machinery, but also higher-order knowledge such as copyrights, documentation, and design specifications. Based in Uttar Pradesh, Scooters India Limited is engaged in not only the manufacture of automobiles, but also their design, R&D, and marketing. By 1975, the organization started rolling out the two-wheeler scooters branded as 'Vijai Super' and 'Lambretta'. The former was targeted to the Indian market, while the latter was manufactured keeping the overseas market in mind. Subsequently, the organization entered the three-wheeler market under the brand name of 'Vikram/Lambro'. In 1997, the organization decided to exit the scooter market, to specifically focus on three-wheelers.

Since its inception, Scooters India Limited has been reporting losses.[2] This continued at least until 1992, when its net worth actually turned negative and the company was declared as sick. We need to understand the conditions under which the organization reported losses since its birth. Scooters India Limited was a result of a joint venture between API, the central government, and Innocenti. However, soon after the organization was founded, Innocenti pulled out of the joint venture. Unfortunately, the entire know-how to Scooters India came from this Italian partner. It realized that transfer of know-how is not sufficient for success. The know-how needs to be installed in the new Indian context as well, for which engineers were not very well equipped. The head, Mr Soundararajan, was a government appointee. He preferred to keep the entire control centralized under him. Also, his ambitious plans led many in the organization to feel that he was more interested in showing a good performance in the short term of five years, the duration for which he had been appointed, rather than actually strengthening the organization during its infancy. His ambitious plans, coupled with emphasis on technology that was not yet accepted in the Indian market, are considered to be the reasons for the continual losses. Subsequent CEOs came from similar backgrounds of government service.

The seeds of turnaround of Scooters India were sown in 1990 when Arun Sahay was appointed as CEO. He had been a veteran in the organization, but had been resisting the closure/sell-off despite government attempts to do so. His emergence as head of the organization is considered the key trigger for turnaround. He would take every step to bridge the gap between management and workers. By moving his office to the factory premises, he was able to connect immediately with the workers. Sahay would ensure that discipline was enforced, which until then, had been deeply influenced and exploited by local politicians for their benefits. To control financial aspects, austerity measures were taken. Promotions were arrested until 1995, and recruitments were frozen (except of a few top management personnel). Another step that led to the reduction of financial burden was the success of the voluntary retirement scheme (though there were some operational issues). Many employees opted for voluntary retirement, and Sahay would ensure that such applications were processed with exceptional speed. At this stage, it is important to underscore the importance of a competent top management team in the successful turnaround of Scooters India. The entire board would involve themselves in the detailed appraisal of the turnaround exercise. There were instances where board members would exploit their external network for the benefit of Scooters India. Because of all these measures, Scooters India Limited finally reported profits in the year 1995–6, and there was no looking back after that.

Illustration II: Ballarpur Industries Limited

Ballarpur Industries Limited (BILT) is another example of a successful turnaround. In this case, the top leader was brought from outside to bring the organization back on track.

The conglomerate was started in the 1920s by Karam Chand Thapar, a first-generation businessman. During his tenure, he had acquired a large number of businesses under the family brand. This helped the conglomerate substantially, given the nationalization scheme of the Government of India, which led to a large number of business portfolios vanishing from the control of the Thapars. Subsequent to K.C. Thapar, his businesses were distributed amongst his four brothers. This was because of a family separation taking place in 2001.

Gautam Thapar was a third-generation businessman, and managed businesses that were under the purview of Brij and Lalit Mohan. His stint with Ballarpur Industries started when he was just thirty-six years old, brought in by Brij and Lalit to take charge. The organization was technically bankrupt at that time, and key personnel had resigned. A detailed diagnosis by Thapar revealed that there was no synchronization between the different functions of the organization. BILT was, at that time in 1996, a sixty-year-old behemoth that operated in the licence raj. There were both deep-rooted malaise and complex leadership issues, not to mention the lack of external focus and agility. The organization had a large number of business divisions under it.

Since the organization had been bankrupt by then, there was immediate need for working capital to keep it afloat. Thapar decided to sell off some of the assets to raise fast cash. There were dynamics that he had to overcome, such as pressure from family members on what and what not to sell. However, given the faith that Brij and Lalit Mohan had in him, he did not have to buckle under any of these views. This helped him, over a period of two years (1997–8), to raise cash and to make the organization leaner. Two businesses were shut down, and voluntary retirement and other forms of retrenchments were implemented.

To tackle issues, he brought in key personnel from another set-up with which he had worked to be a part of this turnaround team. By 1998, the organization began earning profits. However, this did not stop Thapar from strengthening the foundations of this success—after all, there was a huge debt still outstanding. Since the credibility of the organization was being restored, two external financial institutions agreed to participate in the leveraged buyout of the chemical business. This pumped in additional funds into the organization. External professionals were engaged for their expertise in legal, compliance, and other regulatory issues. An assessment of the organizational capabilities revealed that BILT lacked sufficient marketing acumen. To plug this, a new marketing head was brought in, and the result was a strong distribution network. Those who did not comply with the mandates of the turnaround team were shown the door, irrespective of their stature in the organization. This was implemented to such an extent that the paper division's biggest distributor in India was sacked for non-compliance. This action delivered a strong message to the rest of the organization's stakeholders—after all, this distributor was considered so strong that even employees would fear antagonizing him.

As we see, Gautam Thapar confronted the problem of organization decline head-on, and this resulted in a successful turnaround. The top management team included him and other trusted professionals brought from outside. In fact, Thapar was not a part of BILT initially. Hence, the entire top management team may be considered to have been brought from outside. Thapar's leadership was necessary, as this was a family business, and it is easier for owners to trust someone internal when it comes to drastic decision-making. The tool of restructuring was used extensively, and so was financial and operational control.

Illustration III: McDonald's

McDonald's was founded in 1937, and within the next two decades, the organization had established its presence all over the United States. However, by the 1990s, McDonald's profits started to plummet, and in 2003, the organization posted losses for the first time. It was then that a new CEO was brought in, and within a year or so, the organization had been turned around. Analysts attributed poor customer satisfaction and health issues as the reasons for the organizational decline. Another reason that led to the fall of McDonald's was the aggressive expansion plans without any proper control in place. This led to poor operational performance,[3] which translated into customer grievances.

This is a classic case of a quick turnaround. Jim Cantalupo was brought into the ailing organization as the new CEO. Immediately after taking the reins, Cantalupo announced a three-year plan for diametrically changing the fortunes of the organization. Systemic changes were executed, and marketing was done more aggressively. Needless to say, the menu was enhanced to include healthier food items. Operations were streamlined. Rather than expanding by adding more restaurants, the focus was on increasing customer footfalls per restaurant.

CONCLUSION

Turnaround is the phenomenon where a declining organization is steered to a position of profit-earning on a year-on-year basis. To achieve this cherished stage, a sick organization needs to assess and focus on both internal and external aspects—in short, all stockholders. Top leadership is one of the key drivers of an organization's pursuit for turnaround, and different situations mandate different leadership styles during execution. Often, restructuring of the businesses is necessary for changing the organization's fortunes. This may be a painful process, and often leads to mass retrenchment of employees, who are often not at fault for the bad shape of the organization. Needless to say, proper financial and operational controls need to be enforced during the turnaround process to ensure that already scarce resources are not unproductively used. This control presents a paradox, and an organization needs to be very careful as and when these controls are to be enforced and when they are to be relaxed. Overall, a successful turnaround is a war on multiple fronts, and it is the way in which these battles are fought that decides their degree of success.

NOTES

1. Excerpted from http://www.scootersindia.com/html/aboutus_company.htm on 3 September 2010.
2. Maheshwari, S. and Ahlstrom, D. (2004). 'Turning Around a State Owned Enterprise: The Case of Scooters India Limited' *Asia Pacific Journal of Management*, vol. 21, pp. 75–101.
3. Excerpted from http://findarticles.com/p/articles/mi_m3190/is_7_42/ai_n24321263/ on 3 September 2010.

10

Challenges of Leading Growth

INTRODUCTION

In the previous nine chapters, we've discussed the different trajectories that an organization can take to succeed in its pursuit of growth. However, growth sought as a tool for organizational success is one thing—the ability to actually achieve this growth is another. An organization is bound to face difficulties while it aspires to follow a planned route to growth. This can be attributed to factors created by either its competitors or other elements that reside in the business environment. This chapter will discuss the internal factors of an organization that have a tendency to create hurdles in organizational growth.

TRIGGERS THAT IMPEDE GROWTH

Until now, we have discussed ten different strategic tools that organizations can employ to seek growth. Growth is indeed a goal for most organizations. However, there can be instances where growth stagnates (or even becomes negative). We discuss here some of those situations, and offer ways in which the symptoms[1] of such situations can be used to diagnose root problems.

Poor Customer Expectation Management

This is a classic problem that many organizations face. Once an organization realizes it has been able to come up with a value proposition that has been widely accepted in the target segment, it becomes complacent. This may sound harsh, but we find umpteen number of cases where this is a reason for arrested organizational growth.

Once an organization becomes complacent, it loses touch with market realities. Customer preferences change, not only as a function of time, but also as a function of new products/services being introduced in the marketplace. This change in preferences will then automatically result in the attrition of existing customers to other alternatives. This attrition can be a result of multiple scenarios. We enumerate the two most prominent: 1) competitors offering products/services with similar attributes at a lower price to customers; or 2) competitors coming up with products/services with markedly better features at the same price. Both these situations are a sure recipe for the organization's growth plateauing, if not plummeting. The situation becomes all the more grave if managers weaken their grasp on market intelligence. If managers are not connected to the market due to current product/service success, then the situation becomes more problematic—it leads to not only loss of business but also a lack of information for the managers to diagnose why it happened.

Let us now probe a bit deeper into the reasons that would make an organization complacent in the first place. It is possible that an organization has been successful with a particular product line for a long time. Such a context would tempt the organization to believe that this product is ingrained so well in the lives of customers that they have become loyal to it. If another organization comes up with a similar, cheaper product, then the organization tends to feel that customers would reject this new product based on loyalty to its products. But this is seldom the case—if product attributes are comparable, there is no reason for customers to stick to a more expensive product if there are cheaper options available.

Now, let us look at the second prominent reason we have mentioned, as the root cause is very much related to the first reason above. If an organization feels that its value proposition has been well accepted by customers over a substantial period of time, the organization tends to think it is the ultimate version of the product. However, the organization fails to realize that change is the only constant, and this also applies to customer preferences. Similar products with better features may be introduced by competitors, and if they are able to communicate their value proposition to customers more effectively, there is no reason for customers not to shift to this better product. An organization faces such a situation if it stalls in allocating sufficient funds for innovation. Lack of encouragement for innovation will impede an organization from bringing out better variants of the product, thereby giving competitors space. The other cause arises when organizations, convinced of their success, might focus less on R&D. If this is the case, the organization is actually becoming a prisoner of its current success. Other organizations may come up with products that lead to paradigm shifts in the consumption patterns of existing customers, leading to loss of business.

Early Exit from Established Business

Previously, we saw how organizations dig their own grave by staying on with the same product for longer than required, leading to competitors coming in with better value propositions and making this product less sought after in the market. Another situation at the other end of the continuum is a scenario where an organization decides to exit a business line even before earning sufficient profits. The organization must have invested in the entire cycle of business development, starting from product development, channel selection and training, pilot testing of the product, related modifications, and after-sales services (if applicable). The capital expenditure associated with these phases is generally recovered by the organization by staying in said business for a sufficient period. Now, if an organization decides to exit a business even before fully exploiting market potential, then this opportunity to recover the capital expenditure is lost. Needless to say, it is not only recovery of capital expenditure that the organization loses out on, but also the other more scarce resources that had been invested in launching the business line.

The gravity of error by such an early exit is all the more if the abandoned line is the organization's primary source of revenue. By exiting such a business, the organization will surely lose either a 'cash cow' or a 'star' in its portfolio (remember the BCG matrix that was discussed in Chapter 6). Either way, an early exit is taken when an organization believes that the growth in that market has reached a stage of saturation, and no further opportunities are possible. There can be another reason for taking such a faulty decision to exit early—an organization may feel the business is not viable enough because of certain ground-level hurdles. If this is the reason to exit, the organization is actually mixing strategic-level and tactical-level decisions. Inability to handle an operational hurdle should not be a reason for early exit if there is merit in the strategy of staying in the business.

Now, let us try to understand the reason(s) for an organization to feel that a ground-level hurdle is too cumbersome to solve. We understand that human resource is the key to any organizational success. Hurdles and issues are bound to arise if an organization wants to stay in a business that is profitable enough. However, if there is a relevant talent pool available, then there is no reason why this organization would not be able to tackle the problems that arise out of operations in that business domain. The middle to top management of an organization should have a mix of people who are 1) deeply specialized in a particular business domain, and 2) generalists who have fair expertise in other related, and even unrelated, businesses. Such cross-functional acumen helps an organization to come up with innovative ideas for solving problems. Just a word of caution here—often, it is found that organizations have sufficient manpower that belong to category 1. It takes tolerance for an organization and its employees to realize that generalists are equally valuable for organizational growth, and therefore, should be inducted and given similar career growth options within the organization.

Static Nature of Organizational Capabilities

Once an organization has tasted success, it may feel its existing capabilities are apt for it to win in the game of growth. Such a view is generally reinforced if an organization continues to succeed by following the same routines and other mantras over a substantial period of time. However, this generally leads to subsequent organizational struggle (if not decline), because of reasons discussed below.

One of the reasons a static view can hamper organizational growth is the predictability of its moves. If an organization follows the same heuristics again and again, then it will succeed to the extent that demand in the market exceeds the supply of the value propositions. The moment there is competition between industry players for a fixed piece of the market, the organization with a static view loses out. Other players will easily predict the moves of this organization.

Another reason for the break on organizational growth is if the organization takes a static view of its capabilities. These capabilities must have been useful at some earlier point of time—in fact, the organization would have definitely tasted huge success over a long time span by housing these capabilities. However, the organization needs to take cognizance of the fact that the business environment is ever-changing. As a result, these capabilities should be dynamic in nature to meet the demands of the ever-changing environment. Otherwise, these capabilities face obsolescence. Let us take an example to understand this. Consider an instance of a long-standing, successful organization which has deep expertise in consumables and distributing these products through its vast distribution channels. This distribution capability has been giving the organization growth and success on a year-on-year basis. Such a historic track record of success tends to give this organization a feeling that this distribution capability will continue to help the organization grow in the future as well. However, the environment is ever-changing. The Internet and mobile phones have deeply integrated themselves in the lifestyles of the common man. Such environmental dynamics may alter the very purchasing pattern of consumers, and in fact, customers may feel it more convenient to order utility products through either the Internet or mobile phones. Such a shift in consumer preference for the purchase channel will then make the distribution capability of this organization redundant. Alterations in this distribution capability may give a competitive advantage, but the organization needs to actively realize the need for modifications in capabilities, rather than maintaining the notion that its existing capability set is sufficient for growth, irrespective of changes in the environment.

Legacy of Old Leadership

Leadership is an essential component that decides the destiny of an organization. As an organization matures, and/or its business environment changes, the way in which it needs to be steered also changes. This may require the leadership to take a very different view of its own role, or may even require a paradigm shift in management. But there may be organizations that have been successful under a particular leader, or a particular style of leadership. This might have continued for a substantial duration, leading to a feeling that this leader (or the leadership style) is best for the organization. However, this need not be true all the time. Changing times mandate change in the leadership style for organizational success. But the organization may feel, often not rightly so, that past success of a particular leadership style is a sufficient reason for it to succeed in changing times. As we discussed in brief, there can be two instances where existing leadership may not be best: 1) a marked changed in environment; or 2) a change in organizational life cycle. Let us throw further light on both these possibilities.

Environmental attributes have an impact on the route that an organization should take for sustained growth. For example, if there is substantial availability of resources in the environment compared to the requirement of organizations (that is, munificence in the environment), then the focus of a prudent organization should be in attempting to maximize the output and sales of end-products. A strong, sales-driven leadership seems apt for an organization in such a situation. However, if there is a scarcity of the same relevant resources, then prudence would require an organization to focus more on efficient utilization of those resources internally. This would require a strong, operations-driven leadership, which would put proper controls in place. A third scenario can be an environment that is characterized by high dynamism and uncertainty. An organization situated in this environment would require leadership that can make fast decisions to exploit opportunities as they unfold, plus have the vision to predict future market movements. Recessionary times would require an organization to have charismatic leadership, so employees and other stakeholders stick with the organization, even if this means forgoing immediate pay-outs.

Just like environmental attributes, the life-cycle stage of an organization is also an important factor that decides the suitability of relevant leadership styles. During the inception of an organization, systems and processes are almost non-existent. The leader would be required to undertake the challenge of defining the culture, as well as the vision and mission. Also, the leadership would be required to focus more on *exploration*—be it the exploration of different businesses that the organization can venture into, or be it the exploration of different avenues for tapping talent pools. Over time, the organization matures and processes stabilize. At this stage, an organization is expected to earn profits and break even as early as possible. The leadership at this stage needs to focus more on *exploitation*—be it the exploitation of different ventures that the organization has moved into, or exploitation of resources (including human resources) for the maximum possible benefit of the organization. Just because a leader (or a particular style of leadership) succeeded in building the foundation of an organization at its inception does not mean the leader would be equally successful in the maturity phase of the organization. The shareholders then need to take a tough call on changing the leadership depending on the life-cycle stage of the organization.

Capital Crunch

To run a business, an organization needs to invest capital. Most times, the hard cash put in by the owners is not sufficient to venture into new businesses, or even expand existing businesses. This requires an organization to raise capital from the market. There are different sources of external funds. For example, an organization may float bonds and attract individuals to buy those bonds (terms and conditions similar to fixed deposits offered by banks) by offering better returns on those bonds. Another source of such external funds can be financial institutions (such as banks), which may be approached for loans. The above two sources are often clubbed together to be termed as external debt. The acid test while seeking such funds is the perception of the project (in the minds of the prospective lenders) in terms of viability and risk. If the perceived risk is high, then the expected return (that is, interest rate) on the invested funds will also be high. This may make borrowing expensive, and repayment of interest may excessively eat into the profits from such a venture. This phenomenon has a positive side as well—if an organization has a recurring liability to pay interest, then controls are put in place to ensure that there is strong financial discipline.

Another channel for raising capital is by floating shares. By selling shares, an organization can raise the necessary capital for a project or business venture. Since there is no binding in terms of interest payments, profits from the venture remain undivided. Also, by taking this route the capital structure changes (higher equity-to-debt ratio) and as a result, there are better chances of raising debt at a later date (for a different project). But issuing new shares generally dilutes the ownership pattern of existing shareholders, and the latter may resist such channels for raising funds. Also, if the enhanced base of shareholders demands dividends (as compared to capital appreciation) as a mode of payout, this may deplete the organization's reserves and surpluses.

Having understood the different challenges an organization faces in its growth path, we now graduate to an illustration of a few cases that will help us gain insights on how such impediments actually come in the path of real-life organizations.

ILLUSTRATIONS

Illustration I: SEWA Trade Facilitation Centre (STFC)[2]

The parent organization of STFC is the Self Employed Women's Association (SEWA). To understand the growth challenges for STFC, a brief understanding of its evolution is necessary. SEWA has an affluent heritage of providing livelihood to several poor rural families in Gujarat and other states. The organization worked for the betterment of the rural poor, providing employment opportunities to rural women through utilizing their skills in an appropriate manner, supporting them to earn their livelihood through a respectable and exploitation-free approach. The gracious work carried out by SEWA in various categories had its own distinctive standing in the consumer market.

The STFC initiative was the derivative of a similar noble cause by SEWA, and recently accomplished a Rs 5 crore turnover mark. The SEWA Trade Facilitation Centre, as a business organization, was one of a kind; it was formed by more than 15,000 rural artisan-shareholders from the remote districts of north Gujarat. The initiative that started by providing a platform to rural artisans gradually transformed itself into a profitable venture, primarily owned by the rural poor producers. The company provided an opportunity to poor rural women to utilize their artistic skills in a profitable business enterprise. Dissimilar to other organizations, STFC supported its social objective through a principle that 60 percent of the total production cost of every product would go to the artisans as income. In the entire supply chain, every function is performed by artisans—cloth is woven by weavers, printed by block printers, cutting and stitching done by tailors or daughters of garment workers. Over the years, STFC marked its presence across 200 villages forming sixty groups, comprising 3500 women artisan members. The objective was to provide livelihood to poor rural women in Gujarat who were badly affected by the earthquake in 2001. The pillars of the company were rural women who possessed the superior skill of producing handmade embroidered products. The task for STFC was to provide fair compensation to the underprivileged rural women through leveraging their skills in a productive manner.

The business strategy of STFC operations revolved around marketing and supply chain management. The major focus of the company remained on supplying raw materials and designs to the rural artisans, procuring finished products from them, and selling these products in domestic and overseas markets. STFC dealt in several product categories, including retail sales at its store and catering to wholesale bulk orders. The company offered a versatile range of products that catered to different strata of society.

The vision of leaders at SEWA was to make STFC products the first name in embroidery. However, it was easier said than done. The major challenge for them was selling more art and artisan skill, not merely a product, per se.

Unlike other industries, the fashion industry was discrete and dynamic. Rapid changes in fashion, newer manufacturing technologies, innovation in designs, and proper understanding of consumers' tastes and preferences were some of the key characteristics of the fashion and lifestyle industry. Understanding market trends, competition from the organized and unorganized players were a concern for STFC. The leadership was aware of the distinctive characteristics of the fashion and lifestyle industry. They were aware that the task for them was difficult and that success in the industry would depend largely on having the right marketing strategy and its effective implementation.

Over the years, the Indian fashion industry witnessed a major shift. With the entry of organized players in the market, the Indian embroidery products that were predominantly sold in domestic markets started to gain international significance. Indian apparel exports gradually started to be looked upon as lucrative, with several producers jostling for position. However, owing to the momentary trends in the fashion industry, technological innovations, product efficiency, and production time played an important role for doing business in the overseas markets. The entry of organized players split the embroidery market into two categories: handmade embroidered products and the high-precision, competitively priced, machine-made products. For handmade product manufacturers similar to STFC there was direct competition from machine-made products along with other handmade products. The major advantages that resulted in the prominence of machine-made products were high speed production, precise work, and competitive pricing. Harmonizing similar attributes was a complex task for producers of handmade products, restricting them from scaling up their business in a significant manner.

As we see here, the existing capabilities of SEWA are no longer sufficient to give the organization a competitive edge over others operating in the fashion industry. Thus, there is a need for dynamically altering these organizational capabilities to suit the changing environment. Also, the leadership is the same as that of the senior personnel of SEWA. Now, STFC operates in a very different context, wherein end-consumers are highly sensitive about the quality and brand of the product that they purchase. The leadership style in one context may not be apt for replication in another.

Illustration II: Enron

We now discuss, in the case of Enron, how an attempt to transform a traditional economy organization into a new-generation one failed. Enron was conceived in 1985 as a result of a merger between two gas pipeline organizations.[3] The initial three–four years of Enron were tough, and every new environmental change nearly endangered its very existence. This made the organization contemplate the decision of changing its very business model—from gas pipelines to energy trading. While doing this, there was focus on related businesses as well, such as building power plants and gas pipelines in other countries. In the 1990s, EnronOnline was launched. This was an Internet-based trading platform that resulted in a massive increase in the volume of energy trading. In a bid to grow, the organization started encouraging employees to innovate for new business generation. The encouragement was to such an extent that new business ideas were made to pass through minimal screening gates, and would often lead to creation of new entities: special purpose vehicles. Enron would then pass off the debt from its balance sheet to these subsidiaries and partnerships.

It is important to note that during the entire period, their CEO was Kenneth Lay. He was succeeded by Jeffrey Skilling in 2001, and within a year, the organization filed for bankruptcy. It is understood that the initial few years were tough. It was this tough time that forced the leadership to steer the organization in a different direction altogether. Later, the organization realized there was scope for related diversification (new market, same/similar product). But the new routes led to substantial bleeding of organizational resources. Subsequent efforts to hide losses only made things worse, and finally, within a short span of time, a mammoth organization (and an icon in the business world) had to shut down.

Illustration III: General Electric (GE)

Having seen an illustration where an organization failed to meet the challenges posed by a growth trajectory, let us embark on another case that will help us understand the way in which an organization succeeds in addressing growth related challenges. GE faced similar environmental turmoil around 2001; however, the way it steered itself clear and succeeded in the pursuit of growth is commendable. The environmental turmoil comprised the 9/11 terrorist attack and subsequent slowdown. To make matters worse, business behemoths the size of Enron and a few others reported huge losses. The latter was, to an extent, because these organizations had to file for bankruptcy and serious corporate governance issues were raised. The stakeholders raised issues on GE similar to those of Enron, given the complex business practices in which they were both involved. This led regulatory authorities to make reporting norms more stringent and granular.

Jeffery Immelt succeeded Jack Welch as the CEO of GE in September 2001.[4] The initial period was not very comfortable, given the non-conducive business environment, and the legacy of an iconic leader like Welch. One key agenda that Immelt followed was to increase transparency within the organization. This required him to restructure some of the functions and subsidiaries and alter the very communication tactics previously followed. Without compromising on the acquisition spree, Immelt refocused on organic growth.

Needless to say, the twenty-first century witnessed the advent of a scenario where emerging economies started becoming a coveted destination for fast-track growth. GE did not let this opportunity go and made its presence felt in a big way in the healthcare industries of India and China. This phenomenon of being globally present in a way the local way of thinking is utilized has also been referred to as glocalization. These markets were idiosyncratic, in the sense that customers here were price sensitive, but not at the cost of reduced quality. As a result, GE had to think of innovative ways to reduce the cost of its products without compromising on performance.

There was another phenomenon that these markets were witnessing. Traditional organizations in these economies were becoming big, and would soon start operating in developed economies where global organizations like GE had a stronghold. To pre-empt such a move, GE introduced these improved cost-benefit products in their home markets. This has been referred to in the literature as reverse innovation.[5] Otherwise, the emerging economy behemoths would have introduced similar products in the developed nations, seeing a vacuum for such products there.

CONCLUSION

Growth is a direction most organizations seek, but it brings with it many challenges. Customers are the most important stakeholders for almost all organizations, and an organization needs to fulfil their expectations well to be able to grow and succeed. Certain environments are ever-changing, as a result of which existing capabilities face early obsolescence. Hence, if an organization is operating in an uncertain and dynamic environment, it needs to develop a special interest in renewing its capabilities to keep pace with external changes. A growth trajectory also requires an organization to alter its leadership style to suit its life-cycle maturity. Finally, an organization needs funds for growth. The way the requirement of funds is fulfilled is an important factor that decides not only the success of a venture but also other strategic parameters such as ownership patterns, prospects of future access to capital, and financial discipline, to name a few.

NOTES

1. For a similar analysis, please refer to the article Olson, M.S., Bever, D., and Verry, S. (2008). 'When Growth Stalls', *Harvard Business Review*, 86 (3), pp. 50–61.

2. Immelt, J.R., Govindarajan, V., and Trimble, C. (2009). 'How GE is Disrupting Itself', *Harvard Business Review*, 87 (10), pp. 56–65.

3. Excerpted from Ghosh, A. and Jaiswal, A. (2009). SEWA Trade Facilitation Centre: Designing Roadmap for Business Expansion, IIMA/BPO329, Case of the Indian Institute of Management Ahmedabad.

4. Excerpted from http://www.iimcal.ac.in/community/finclub/dhan/dhan2/art23-en-pdf on 26 August 2010.

5. Excerpted from http://www.ge.com/company/leadership/ceo.html on 26 August 2010.

11

Leading Growth for Small and Medium Enterprises

INTRODUCTION

Entrepreneurship is not only about individual imagination; it is about building teams to exploit opportunities previously untouched. Entrepreneurs need to manage, minimize, and especially prioritize risks. When small and medium enterprises (SMEs) take the entrepreneurial path, it must be ensured that they have sufficiently robust quantitative models to monitor the market and their internal processes. In the case of family-run businesses, they need to pay attention to professional norms of management. These organizations need to imaginatively raise capital by thinking of new ways of dealing with intellectual property. This chapter attempts to understand entrepreneurial ventures and ways of raising capital for SMEs. Characteristic traits of family-run businesses must also be examined. Three cases will illustrate these concepts: the Royal Orchid Hotel, Naukri.com, and MakeMyTrip.com.

UNDERSTANDING ENTREPRENEURIAL VENTURES

Entrepreneurship—The Key Concept

Entrepreneurship, rather than being the attempt of a single person who starts a new venture, is a team effort where many people come together to support an ideal. It is a myth that entrepreneurship is about big organizations and big realities where big changes take place due to the formidable imagination of a few people. Rather than being a romantic pursuit of huge success drawing upon commitment, fortune, and luck, entrepreneurship is about building teams that can use existing resources in effective ways. Entrepreneurship is characterized by synergy and interdependence rather than by self-reliance and 'do it yourself'. It is about creating spaces where people can coordinate with each other and adhere to the needs of the market.

Challenges in Entrepreneurial Ventures

An important aspect of entrepreneurship is the management of the risks and uncertainties associated with a new venture. These risks are associated with anticipating numerous details like production, development, distribution, and marketing. The risks in each of these functions must be identified, then minimized by the entrepreneur. It is necessary to understand how resources can be used to fuel new methods of functioning so that risks can be identified and prioritized for mitigation.

There are some risks which could jeopardize the entire venture if they are not identified and dealt with properly. Some may pertain to regulatory measures that the government is contemplating. If an understanding of these regulations does not exist, wrong decisions could be taken which could threaten the survival of the venture. The intended market needs to be understood, as wrong assumptions can lead to disastrous consequences. It is therefore important to recognize that certain risks could threaten the very survival of the entrepreneurial venture.

Risks which are slightly less dangerous emerge from lack of resource planning, and could result in resource wastage that increases costs. It is therefore important to be aware of the different ways in which resources could be used and markets could be accessed. After this it is necessary to choose an effective way to function. Wrong decisions could prove costly as it becomes very difficult to change the course of action after the decision has been locked in.

However, not all risks require meticulous planning. There are many which can be easily addressed by simply paying attention. A successful entrepreneur identifies these risks and quickly addresses them. Some may revolve around small operational details in which the entrepreneur needs to be personally involved. Nothing must be left to chance, as things can go wrong in unexpected places. An entrepreneur who pays attention to small details can avoid risks but, if left unaddressed, these same details can also create obstacles for the venture.

Nothing must be taken for granted while launching an entrepreneurial venture. Successful entrepreneurs should evaluate possibilities on the ground, testing various plans that can be used for the business before adopting them. This can then give them the confidence to launch their plans on a bigger scale.

One of the most important constraints for entrepreneurial ventures is the availability of capital. In situations where capital is scarce, it must be used wisely. Capital should not be used impulsively but with care and responsibility. Detailed plans need to be made before investing capital in a particular aspect of the venture. Plans also need to be made to ensure every rupee gives the highest returns.

When pilot surveys or other tests are carried out, new ideas and learning must be obtained. Surveys and research are not about validating initially held ideas, but understanding and exploiting new creative ideas that can emerge. Pilot tests are about discovering hidden aspects of the business and therefore the entrepreneur needs to be learning oriented. The studies are an opportunity to obtain new insights and spot trends that might have been ignored earlier.

These pilot studies need to be planned effectively and all phases and objectives need to be clearly defined. Tests are useless unless their lessons are implemented and their consequences understood. Even the most negative results need to be evaluated with honesty. Ideas may need to be dropped, or the venture may need to be holistically redesigned.

Rather than seeing risks as the basis of obtaining higher returns, it needs to be understood that a planned approach towards addressing risks is more useful. The sources of the risks need to be identified and plans need to be made about how these sources can be dealt with. Tests are not about reinforcing traditional and old beliefs but are about creating new opportunities and insights for the venture.

Entrepreneurship is not only about exciting new ideas but about creating reliable processes and effective rules to implement them. Careful planning leads to efficient procedures for dealing with resources. Entrepreneurial ventures are not about ad hoc decisions but about identifying how people can function as a team and defining the rules for such teams. Rather than being about impulse and imagination, entrepreneurship involves careful analysis, where various scenarios are anticipated. All team members need to know their roles and responsibilities and their expected contributions to the venture. They need to be held accountable for these responsibilities. Rules need to be enforced in the functioning of the venture and a culture of teamwork needs to be fostered.

SOURCES OF CAPITAL FOR SMALL AND MEDIUM ENTERPRISES

SMEs may face constraints in tapping capital from conventional sources. SMEs need to innovate to obtain new sources of capital for the new business designs that they wish to bring to the market, such as sharing licensing and using patents to generate finance. Through these innovative sources, SMEs can create processes of innovation which link capital funding to what happens inside the firm. They can use new sources of capital to fund their entrepreneurial ventures.

SMEs need to think about creative ways of using intellectual property to raise capital. There are specialized firms which have emerged to evaluate the potential of intellectual property, through which SMEs can create innovative business models which help them to mitigate the constraints of capital. Proceeds from the design of new intellectual property could be shared with investors. New ways of trading in intellectual property could be proposed so that ideas are financially leveraged to raise funds.

By collaborating with other firms which specialize in intellectual property, SMEs can better understand the business processes of a product's marketability. Thus knowledge networks emerge which help improve the market validity of intellectual property. This also ensures that the risks associated with an idea are shared by a wide range of players, and that the feasibility of an idea is more carefully scrutinized. It also means that an idea's innovation value has to increase, as many organizations will be competing in the intellectual property market.

SMEs need to develop concepts of the products they want to patent and launch. These concepts are needed to raise capital. They can approach investors who have the potential to evaluate these concepts and contribute to their improvement. Prototypes can then be developed on the basis of these concepts with investor backing. It is the investor who has the knowledge to understand the power of concepts regarding whom SMEs can target.

This means designing new methods of sharing information with investors. SMEs will have to negotiate between maintaining the secrecy of information pertaining to the organization and an investor's need to know. This will mean creating bundles of information around a product which can be used to draw investors, but which don't reveal other aspects of the SME's functions. It also means creating capabilities which can interact with investors on the level of ideas and concepts. It will involve building human resources who are able to liaise with investors about the development of concepts into products. It will also require a new system of relationships which are specific to products and which may not be long term. It means engaging with investors who are going to closely monitor the functioning of the organization where a product is concerned and who are going to have intense information demands regarding these products.

SMEs need to create market forecasts of their products and use these to lure capital. They need to target individual investors who have knowledge of the field and discuss the market possibilities of their products with them. While doing this they can't be reluctant to reveal the progress they have made in the market. This creates an additional responsibility of constant innovation to ensure that they remain ahead of the market. It also involves acknowledging interdependencies through which the SME is willing to accommodate the concerns of investors.

SMEs need to innovate on how value can be created from avenues which have not been previously exploited. They need to demonstrate practical strategies of how value can be created from the concepts being discussed. Rather than investment being a speculative exercise, it becomes a process through which knowledge is evaluated. An SME will need to show flexibility of integrating its product with emerging market trends. It will need to respond to the market by building new models of product deployment.

In order to attract financial capital, SMEs will have to demonstrate intellectual capital that it can deliver. The intellectual capital must articulate its knowledge in the form of practical decisions that will respond to the market. Thus SMEs need to have capabilities where research and development is not merely an isolated, technical function, but is able to understand day-to-day business implications. Similarly, the personnel who raise resources for the SME need to be aware of the technical details of their products. SMEs need to be capable of translating product innovation into business terms, and then again use business inputs to modify the innovation.

The market returns of a product need to be constantly addressed. Investors need the confidence that an SME has constructed a market model which can input new information. SMEs need to demonstrate that they have the dynamic capability of using market input to alter their processes and products. This needs to be done in a relatively short time, as delays can mean loss of competitive advantage.

SMEs will be able to raise capital when they can satisfy investors that they have the capability of responding to the market. Using new information, SMEs should constantly update their market models on the basis of which they are functioning. Learning is an important part of the entrepreneurial venture. When they attempt to tap unexploited opportunities, SMEs must be prepared to constantly learn from them. This learning must be reflected in the understanding of the market. SMEs need to prove that they are nimble and swift in their responses. They must be able to develop quantitative measures which are regularly updated. They need to be methodical in updating these measures and constantly monitoring them. It is these capabilities that will attract investment. It will also enable SMEs to sustain themselves over a long period of time in the face of tough competition. SMEs must be able to translate various quantitative measures in terms of the impact that they have on each other. For instance, the time required for a new breakthrough has an impact on the level of market penetration. So SMEs need to be able to compute such interdependencies quantitatively and constantly take decisions based on anticipated trends.

TRAITS OF A FAMILY BUSINESS

For family-owned businesses to effectively function as entrepreneurial SMEs, they must show exceptional leadership capabilities. The leadership must reflect confidence in professional norms where decisions are taken after careful analysis. Investors and employees must have the confidence that decisions are being taken after responsible analysis. Leadership must be accountable for decisions taken. The systems that it builds must reflect the role of data and should revolve around analysis and reason.

It is the existence of analytical ability that influences the governance capability in family business-owned resources. Governance can only be as good as existing systems. Governance must reflect the importance given to acquiring and monitoring information. It must also give space to the expression of opinion on the basis of the available information, which must be used to predict and forecast scenarios.

Family-owned businesses can sometimes degenerate into situations where employees feel that the family does not have the imagination to take innovative decisions. Therefore family-owned businesses need to avoid situations where decisions are taken purely on the basis of habit. They need to introspect on how their decisions can help the organization to do better in the market. They need to create scenarios to determine how they are faring.

Rather than rely on stereotypes of what does well, family-owned businesses need to constantly assess the firm's priorities. Stereotypes often emerge as vested interests of the family prevents its members from seeing things which are obvious to others. Therefore there needs to be a decision-making culture which does not celebrate the family, but provides room for analysis. The family can at the same time instill values in the organization through personal example, but they need to demonstrate that the business comes before the family and that professionalism is deeply valued.

The entrepreneurial ventures of family businesses can become trapped in the personal passions of the family's business leader. This must be avoided. Management must critically introspect on the entrepreneurial schemes being proposed. Every decision needs to be taken on the basis of management principles rather than on the whims of the managers belonging to the family. Careful attention needs to be paid to sources of information and the logic which supports decisions. Managers from the family need to be more open to criticism in order to make better decisions.

At the same time, the family can inspire the organization to take innovative decisions. This culture of innovation can motivate everyone in the organization to constantly learn. It can help them to contribute to the organization without any inhibition. The family can lay the foundation for a decision-making culture that lays emphasis on values which cannot be compromised.

This can ensure that the business does not simply follow the trends and fashions of the market, but has certain core values on the basis of which it makes decisions. This means that the organization retains its ability to be different from others and take courageous decisions. This ability can help greatly in sustaining the culture of entrepreneurship. It also means that people in the organization learn the ability to mitigate the risks inherent in their decisions. This is effective risk management that can lead to the organization's success.

The family can become a reference on the norms of behaviour in the organization. People take cues from the family on the values that they must emphasize and others that they must shun. Thus the family can become the basis of an entrepreneurial spirit where each decision must be justified on the basis of the returns that it can bring to the organization. These decisions can determine the need for constantly updating information about what is happening in the market. This constant monitoring of information from the market can lead to modifications in products and processes that help the organization to do well.

Managers from the family can demonstrate the need to think carefully before simply following current fashions in business. As a result, other managers in the organization also acquire the ability to think creatively and focus on the need to innovate. The organization becomes a place where people feel the need to constantly learn and innovate and integrate these innovations with the broader strategy. They begin to lead the market rather than follow it. Managers from the family can also tune themselves into unorthodox sources of information which they can use to alter the processes of the organization.

Rather than seeing the processes of management as inhibiting innovation, family-owned businesses need to strengthen decision-making on the basis of professional management. It is the tightly held tenets of professional management that can help an organization to focus and develop innovations in areas in which it has the capacity to do so. The principles of management render a beneficial discipline to constantly improve. Improvements can emerge from surprising sources if people are allowed to try new things. They are confident that if there is a gap in what they are proposing, someone else will point out the error and the organization will benefit.

Management processes reflect the building of rules and procedures which can guide people in making decisions where rules of thumb which emerge from proven practices in the market can be created, building on decision-making processes which have proven successful. At the same time, the decision-making process must reflect ground realities rather than the legacy of the family. This reforms the decisions that the organization needs to take today rather than be trapped by the inertia of the family's past legacy.

Managers from the family can reflect a new leadership that is willing to introspect on its decisions without being defensive. When managers from the family do this, other managers soon follow suit. Rather than the family becoming a force of inertia, it can become a source of constant innovation. It can reflect a vision that shows the ability to take risks.

We now explore three ventures through real-life cases.

ILLUSTRATIONS

Illustration I: Royal Orchid[1]

The founder of Royal Orchid, Chender Baljee, reflects a study in perseverance.[2] He knows that the very process of obtaining the approvals to establish a hotel in India can be a long process. Various clearances must be obtained from different government ministries. And then there is the need to engage with labour unions and workers so that the hotel can function successfully. Human resources are an important competitive advantage in the service industry, especially during recession, when there is a need to hold on to the best human resources as business slows.

The first Royal Orchid hotel opened in Bengaluru in 1973. Today, Royal Orchid operates thirteen business and leisure hotels in six cities. For financial year 2009–10, Royal Orchid hotels turned a profit of Rs 697.51 lakh. One of their largest costs was their employees, totalling Rs 2382.62 lakh, indicating the emphasis that the organization places on nurturing its human resources. While promoters hold about 70 percent of the share of the organization, they have been able to raise resources from the market for their entrepreneurial ventures such as opening new hotels. Of the paid share capital of Rs 2723.4 lakh, public shares are about 30 percent.

But Royal Orchid has not stopped its entrepreneurial ventures. It plans to open three more hotels—in Hyderabad, Jaipur, and Navi Mumbai. Also, its entrepreneurial plans are not restricted to merely expanding to new cities. They extend to providing facilities such as Wi-Fi which ensures that they are able to serve their guests in the best possible way, adding to their brand image. They also interface with celebrities to ensure that various events take place in Royal Orchid hotels to keep the brand in the public eye.

Illustration II: Naukri.com

Naukri.com represents a refreshing attempt at using the internet to cater to the job market and to create opportunities for both employers and employees. Naukri.com is an entrepreneurial venture that focuses on providing services to job seekers by providing information about openings. It attempts to bridge information asymmetries in the labour market by constantly keeping people updated about trends. It has now generated a vast pool of candidates who are on the lookout for a job and can cater to employers by helping them make the right choice. At a time when many dot-com companies had gone bust, naukri.com generated a sustainable revenue model by catering to job seekers.

Sanjeev Bhikchandani founded naukri.com in 1995 and Info Edge (India) Limited[3] went public in 2006, listed on the Bombay stock exchange as well as National Stock Exchange. Apart from offering services to employers and job seekers, it diversified into other sectors such as matrimony, real estate, and education. When naukri.com launched in 1997, it received an investment of Rs 7.29 crore from the ICICI Information Technology Fund. It thus demonstrated that if an appropriate business model and concept could be developed, then even an entrepreneurial venture could raise capital. At the heart of this venture are the core values of customer satisfaction, entrepreneurship, knowledge, results, and trust.

For the first quarter of financial year 2010–11, the company reported a profit after tax of Rs 173 million. This was an increase of 30 percent over the profits of the previous year—Rs 133 million. Increases in expenses were largely due to higher staff expenses, indicating the emphasis the company placed on human resources.

The company had raised Rs 1703 million through an IPO in 2006 and over 9200 shareholders. naukri.com employs 1600 people and functions in thirty-three cities.

Illustration III: MakeMyTrip.com[4]

MakeMyTrip.com represents an interesting entrepreneurial venture of bringing airlines and passengers together to leverage the opportunities that exist from the needs of people to travel. MakeMyTrip.com attempts to offer exciting opportunities and facilities to travellers, while expanding the businesses of the airlines in the transport industry. It provides a platform through which airlines and passengers can obtain information and make decisions. Airlines can make revenue management decisions about appropriate ticket pricing, while passengers can make plans about their travel. Thus MakeMyTrip.com has been able to tap a business opportunity by catering to the needs of both airlines and passengers.

It not only provides airline tickets but also information about other transport facilities and hospitality facilities such as hotels. Through this, customers can make the best use of their money while making travel plans. Deep Kalra founded the company in 2000, and while the company first focused on the India–US travel market, it has now diversified into various other routes and sectors. MakeMyTrip.com also nurtured its franchisees in order to add to its brand. It has been helped by investors and private equity firms that allowed it to raise capital, and it consults them while taking major business decisions. Among the values that MakeMyTrip. com cherishes are customer centricity, accountability, innovation, and teamwork.

In August 2010, MakeMyTrip (India) Private Limited decided to list itself on the NASDAQ. The capital raised by the company would be used for strategic expansion. It also intended to enhance its technology so that it could innovate further and offer new services. It was this spirit of entrepreneurship that made MakeMyTrip the largest online travel company in India. The company had access to 4000 hotels through which it could provide hotel bookings to customers.

CONCLUSION

Even small and medium enterprises can succeed and do well if they show sufficient entrepreneurial spirit. They can raise capital and expand and become public companies. These organizations need to develop sound concepts and need to constantly monitor the market for new opportunities. They need to reduce the risks involved in business and keep looking for avenues of innovation. They need to show the confidence to expand to new locations. At the same time, they must also expand to new services through which they can leverage business opportunities. Entrepreneurial firms need to show a learning orientation so that they constantly improve. It is only through constantly improving efficiency and paying attention to market analysis that entrepreneurial ventures can succeed.

NOTES

1. Excerpted from http://www.royalorchidhotels.com/pdf/quarter-30-06-10.pdf on 23 August 2010.
2. Excerpted from http://knowledge.wharton.upenn.edu/india/article.cfm?articleid=4375 on 23 August 2010.

3. Excerpted from http://www.infoedge.in/corporate-overview.asp on 23 August 2010.
4. Excerpted from http://www.makemytrip.com/about-us/company_profile.php on 23 August 201.

12

Leading Growth through Turbulent Times

INTRODUCTION

Organizations must attempt to understand different environmental characteristics and craft detailed plans of response to anticipated changes by suitably modifying their processes and use of resources. They must also be willing to make changes in chosen markets in order to adapt and maintain environmental stability. They must not only exploit new opportunities but also build a reserve of resources to bear any environmental shocks. They must build capabilities to obtain greater information about the environment, and anticipate scenarios based on indicators from the environment. We will discuss three cases of how organizations were able to manage turbulent environments to emerge as successful businesses—the State Bank of India, Southwest Airlines, and Hewlett-Packard. These illustrations indicate how innovation and careful business analysis need to be combined for an organization to successfully manage a turbulent environment.

ENVIRONMENTAL ATTRIBUTES—WHAT CONSTITUTES TURBULENCE?

Environments represent the context in which organizations function, and the uncertainties with which an organization must engage. Environments are dynamic contexts which represent changes in the political, economic, and social landscapes within which organizations have to adapt. But environments also contain the resources which organizations can exploit for their advantage. Environments contain complex resource chains for which many organizations compete. A proper understanding of the environment is essential if organizations are to survive turbulent times.[1]

In unstable times, it becomes difficult for organizations to predict environmental changes. Therefore, they must plan for multiple scenarios, and be ready to adapt to unforeseen changes. Within each scenario, they must be ready for contingencies to which they can respond. Careful planning ensures that organizations are not afraid of large-scale changes that may occur in the environment. Organizations will then be ahead of their competitors in their ability to react to environmental changes such as an economic crisis.

A crisis in the environment is identified by an unexpected scarcity of resources. Organizations must plan for changing future levels of resource availability and formulate strategies of how they will run their businesses in these different times. Such plans must not only pertain to changes in organizational processes, but must integrate these processes with the market. The demand for products and services may suddenly fall, and organizations must not only look for early signals which indicate such fall in demand but must also plan what they will do if and when this happens.

Organizations must also obtain information about other organizations in the same sector. Using this information, they must be able to assess how other organizations will react to changes in resources and markets. They must be able to model the behaviour of competitors to changes in input and output markets. Organizations must acquire information not only about competitors in their sector but also of other organizations in the resource chain. Such information can help them to analyse how different organizations will behave during times of environmental turbulence.

Stable environments can enable organizations to form long-term plans which they can execute without many changes. Unstable environments mean that organizations must be ready to change their strategic plans in short time spans. Organizations must simulate environmental scenarios to be able to adapt to the conditions. Unstable environments don't mean that organizations simply react in an ad hoc manner to changes in the environment. They must be able to identify and foresee which parts of the environment can be uncertain, and for each uncertainty, they must have an action plan ready. Thus organizations must have the vision to craft plans that will help them to do well in different environmental conditions.

While dealing with unstable environments, organizations may feel that they are not be in control, that they have to simply go by what is happening in the environment and learn from their mistakes. Yet organizations need to understand that mistakes can still be avoided if they are able to simulate scenarios and constantly update them using available information. They also need to understand what different actors such as suppliers and distributors are doing in the market. This information needs to be incorporated into simulated scenarios.

While organizations need to respond to changes in the environment, they must have a clear plan of what they will do in different environmental conditions. An organization must anticipate potential outcomes by building different scenarios. If it missed some information while building a scenario, and the actual reality turns out to be different, then the organization must learn to include this information the next time round. It is by building such information capabilities that an organization can do well in unstable environments. An organization needs to be able to anticipate different scenarios in areas where it doesn't have accurate information, and needs to improve its planning capabilities by comparing these scenarios with the present reality.

When an organization takes a decision on the spur of the moment, it must not be impulsive. It must have already had a plan about what to do when certain signals emerged from the environment. It needs to make the decisions about the course it will follow when the environmental conditions become adverse. Changes to the original plan arise if the organization obtains additional information about the environment. And the organization must have decided what to do in the event of such additional information.

This does not mean that an organization is not flexible in its strategic plans. If a change to the strategic plan can result in the organization exploiting opportunities in the environment, then the organization must make these changes. But the changes must be backed by a detailed analysis of expected consequences. The organization must be clear about what it seeks to achieve. The organization can alter its expectations, but any downturn should have been anticipated as a part of the analysis of the environment.

If the environment is unstable, organizations can be flexible about their goals, but they must not reduce the number of goals. They must build models which can predict what will be achieved in particular environmental situations. They must be able to predict what they will be able to achieve given the worst environmental circumstances. At the same time, they must be honest in assessing what they may be able to achieve. They must not include performances below potential in the formulation of goals. In these situations, a better performance can lead to a sense of complacency, as the original target was based on the assumption of underperformance.

If the environment is unstable, organizations must improve their technologies and processes to suit the environment. They must have a menu of possible responses to the changing environment, be able to decide which means to adopt, and they must develop the capabilities to implement these technologies without confusion. It is the unwillingness to change technologies and processes that leads to poor performance in unstable environments.

THE CONCEPT OF FIT

An organization may decide to set many targets for itself. If it is able to achieve these targets in an unstable environment, it has *fit* itself to the needs of the environment. This reflects the capability of the organization to use the environment for its growth. Every environmental condition represents an opportunity, and the organization must be able to recognize and use that opportunity.

Apart from targets, another important aspect is the processes adopted by an organization. Processes must reflect the collection of information and their analysis in ways which satisfy environmental requirements. Organizations must have multiple points through which they collect information about the environment. They must compare different sources of information to find out if there are any differences between these indicators. Over a period of time, they must be able to build reliable methods of accessing information.

Processes are also about acquiring resources from the environment. An organization must be able to anticipate the different levels of resources that the environment can provide. It must be able to calculate what contributes to the cost of the resources and be able to plan its actions on the basis of the cost of resources. When processes have been able to adapt to the cost of resources, the organization has been able to fit itself to the environment.

The technologies and methods of functioning must be flexible to the needs of the environment. The organization must have the ability to change its technologies and processes to adapt. Rigidities can constrain the actions that an organization can take. However, flexibility must be applied on the basis of sound plans and analysis. An organization must not change its method of functioning just because of a market trend. Fit is not about doing what everyone else does. Fit is about achieving goals in a given environment, and implementing processes that are able to adapt to the needs of the environment.

While there is no need to simply follow the processes of other organizations in the environment, there is a need to set a benchmark for best practices. These best practices reflect the ways in which other organizations have achieved fit within the environment. The organization needs to compare its practices with the best practices, and strive to improve its processes. The pursuit of excellence based on the values of the organization must involve an awareness of the changes taking place in management technologies. Detailed analysis based on reliable and valid information is an effective way of adjusting to dynamic environments.

The environment represents the different forms of interdependencies an organization must scrutinize in order to achieve success. No organization can be completely self-reliant, nor can it be bothered about its interest alone. Organizations too caught up with their self-interest soon find the environment unable to sustain their growth. Fit is about calculating the interdependencies in the environment to ensure that organizations are able to grow in different conditions. Not paying attention to these interdependencies can lead to incorrect assumptions about the market, and great losses in the long run. It was not paying sufficient attention to the interdependencies in the environment that led to the Great Depression in the earlier part of the twentieth century and the sub-prime crisis in the twenty first century.

Fit is understanding how organizational actions affect interdependencies in the environment. Based on changes in these interdependencies, the environment also changes. The organization must be able to read these changes in the environment. Many times organizations are not able to understand the different indicators of change. It is in understanding the comprehensive nature of indicators in the environment that an organization can achieve fit. For instance, an organization selling consumer goods must be interested in wage trends in the labour market, as the purchasing power of the consumers is based on these trends.

Fit is not about the performance of organizations within a specific sector of the environment. These performances could be temporary phenomena like that of the dot-com companies before the bubble burst around the turn of the millennium. Fit is about a sustainable way of doing business through which an organization is able to constantly anticipate movements in the environment. The successful monitoring of the environment is decided by how organizations depend on each other in the environment—partnerships need to be formed to do well in unstable environments.

An organization's environment is influenced by the decisions that the organization takes. Fit means the organization is accurately able to assess the impact that its decisions will have on the environment. Then the organization can carefully plan its strategy and anticipate the results of its decisions. Even in the face of incomplete information, an organization must develop the capability of quick decision-making. Waiting for more information to make an urgent decision means a lost opportunity, because by that time the environment may have changed, and it may be too late to make a decision.

In the face of incomplete information, organizations must function with a limited set of indicators. They must constantly monitor the environment and analyse the relationships between indicators. Organizations must build indicators for inputs, processes, and outputs. They must know the nature of the relationships between these indicators, and while these indicators may be limited, they will still represent a fairly accurate picture of the environment. The ability to take quick decisions can be built by monitoring these indicators regularly. This will take effort and a learning orientation among the members of the organization. Information and its analysis plays a very important role in an organization achieving fit with its environment.

THE DELICATE BALANCE BETWEEN INTERNAL AND EXTERNAL FIT

External fit refers to the ability of an organization to spot opportunities emerging in the environment. Once these opportunities have been spotted, the organization moves in quickly to exploit them. It beats its competitors in identifying these opportunities and makes use of them for improving its competitive advantage. The organization is able to spot opportunities in the resource chains and in the market, and make best use of them. The organization needs to develop a high degree of analytical capability for spotting these opportunities from the existing information. Intuition is unlikely to help organizations, as it may be based on wrong assumptions and may lead to unsustainable plans in the long run.

Internal fit is the ability of an organization to develop resources and processes that are able to absorb changes in the environment. The organization has the resources to see through tough times, and is able to sustain itself until the environment is more favourable. The organization does not panic and take knee-jerk actions during adverse environmental conditions, but has already planned how to deal with them. It has set in place processes that can help it respond to the crisis. Rather than being caught unawares, the organization has carefully planned for the crisis and has a range of alternatives in place.

The organization needs to combine both internal and external fit. It needs to be quick in spotting opportunities in the environment and at the same time needs to have the resources and processes to absorb changes. Having an extremely good internal fit can slow the organization in responding to opportunities in the market. It can lead to a lack of focus on internal processes that can withstand adverse environmental conditions. The organization can simply forget to build reserves of resources to help it to withstand turbulent environments.

The combination of internal and external fit is achieved by setting up different functional teams within the organization, but to build strategies for internal and external fit can lead to conflicts within the organization. Both of these functional teams can develop vested interests around certain resources and conflict with each other. Rather than working for the organization, they may work for themselves and fail in making the organization environmentally responsive. They view the same information from different perspectives, and lack an integrated vision.

It is therefore necessary to build a set of indicators which convey information about internal and external fit at all levels of the organization. All functional teams in the organization must be asked to factor in these indicators while taking decisions. Thus the awareness of the indicators that are important for the organization is inculcated in all organizational members. They then take decisions based on how these indicators will be affected. A coordinated strategy will ensure a level at which these indicators need to be maintained, as well as the relationships between them. This will ensure that everyone knows the decisions they need to take in order to keep the indicators within acceptable limits.

ART OF STRATEGIC RESPONSE TO ENVIRONMENTAL TURBULENCE

A link needs to be made between different actions, processes, and the results that the organization expects. Organizational performance is important, and therefore its financial and market performance always needs to be kept in mind. The organization needs to demonstrate innovative capabilities in responding to turbulence, as tried-and-tested ideas don't work in dynamic environments. While designing innovative plans, the organization must carefully think about how these plans will impact performance. Consequences in terms of costs and benefits need to be carefully thought through.

Innovation appears to be fraught with many uncertainties and risks. Therefore organizations simply follow the market during turbulent times rather than taking innovative decisions. But conventional approaches don't work, and therefore organizations sink along with the market, rather than standing apart and bucking market trends. Organizations are afraid of innovations because they don't have effective models of how inputs, processes, and outputs interact with each other. Once organizations are able to build effective models for these interactions, they can factor in the impact of the proposed innovations.

Constant innovation means that the organization has been able to build strong information models to understand the environment. The organization is able to effectively understand the input and output markets and is able to build processes to deal with changes in both. These processes enable the organization to spot opportunities in both markets and exploit them for its benefit. These innovations help the organization to stay ahead of the competition in responding to the environment. The organization is no longer afraid of changes in the environment, but is able to use these changes to gain competitive advantage.

Rather than separating creativity and analysis, they need to be integrated. An organization needs to build capabilities to ensure that creativity and business analysis are not performed by different people, as this only creates the potential for conflicts. On the other hand, these functions need to be integrated and performed by the entire strategic team. The organization needs to be creative in responding to the environment and at the same time needs to understand the business implications of its decisions. All decisions need to be made on the basis of the way in which they will impact organizational performance.

Organizations need to build synergies between innovation and business analysis if they are to do well in turbulent environments.

This requires an emphasis on what is constantly happening in the environment and spotting opportunities. These opportunities need to be transformed into concrete and detailed business plans to ensure they are effectively implemented. For such detailed business plans to be formed quickly, the organization must have the capabilities to obtain the required information and analyse it. At the end of the day, it is effective information and analysis management that can help an organization to do well in turbulent environments.

We now illustrate these concepts through three cases—State Bank of India (SBI), Southwest Airlines, and Hewlett-Packard.

ILLUSTRATIONS

Illustration I: State Bank of India (SBI)

The State Bank of India (SBI)[2] has seen many changes in its environment and has done exceedingly well to adapt to them and emerge as the largest state-owned banking and financial services organization in India. In British India, the State Bank of India was known as the Imperial Bank of India and its roots can be traced to the establishment of the Bank of Calcutta in 1806. SBI witnessed many changes in its environment, including the emergence of independent India and its transformation into a public sector institution. SBI used this environmental change to its advantage and built a strong human resource base and was able to attract the best talent. It was able to reach across India, including rural areas, and has the largest number of branches of any bank in the country—around 16,000.

With an asset base of USD352 billion and USD285 billion in deposits, SBI accounts for around one-fifth of all loans given in the country. It has also been able to reach many non-resident Indians and in 2009, had 131 overseas offices spread across thirty-two countries. SBI has been able to adapt to the environmental changes introduced due to economic liberalization by the Indian government in 1991. It has introduced voluntary retirement schemes to deal with the problems of overstaffing, while retaining the best human resources. It has diversified into various financial services—mutual funds, life insurance, credit cards—and even has a capital markets arm.

Through turbulent shifts, SBI has built a wide range of products such as investment banking, consumer banking, asset management, credit cards, and commercial and retail banking. It had a profit of USD2.87 billion and employed approximately three lakh people.[3] Trust is a very important characteristic for a bank to do well. SBI has carefully built its brand in the market with *Forbes* describing it as the tenth most reputed company in the world.[4] In order to raise resources for the many new products it has launched, SBI has raised funds from the stock market by selling its equity.

Illustration II: Southwest Airlines

Southwest Airlines[5] has sustained the concept of a low-cost airline through extremely turbulent times, even as other airlines such as British Airways have suffered huge losses. Having said that, they have also been involved in conflicts with their employees. Periodic strikes have taken their own toll on these airlines apart from rising fuel costs and economic recession.[6] On the other hand, Southwest Airlines was able to post profits for the thirty-seventh consecutive in 2010. Southwest has been able to sustain a business model of flying to the secondary airports of major cities, and increasing the turnaround time of its airlines.

Southwest only one type of aircraft—Boeing 737s—in its fleet and carried more passengers than any other airline in 2009. Based in Dallas, USA, Southwest had a net income of USD178 million for financial year 2008–9. It had a total assets base of USD14.3 billion and an equity of USD4.95 billion. While other airlines have faced major labour problems with recurrent strikes, Southwest has encouraged a model of employee relations where it is not afraid of dealing with unions. Southwest has one of the most unionized workforces with its pilots, technicians, customer service agents, and flight attendants being represented by their own unions.

Southwest has used extremely smart marketing and promotion tactics to improve its business. When it was threatened with a lawsuit for using the 'Just Plane Smart' concept by Stevens Aviation, which used a similar concept, Southwest decided to settle the issue with an innovative idea. The CEOs of both organizations agreed to a boxing match with the winner taking the right to use the concept.[7] The boxing match not only generated a lot of goodwill for both organizations, but also raised some money for charity. The company uses a lot of humour in its advertisements and has succeeded in maintaining its business model through rough times.

Illustration III: Hewlett-Packard

Hewlett-Packard, founded in 1938 in a garage by two electrical engineers from Stanford with an initial capital of USD538, is today one of the largest information technology companies. Over the years, HP has taken up manufacturing of various computing devices such as PCs, servers, storage devices, printers and other imaging products. It has dealt with turbulent environments with a variety of strategic initiatives. These initiatives involved a merger with Compaq in 2002.

Other strategic initiatives involved spin-offs—Agilent Technologies in 1999—and acquisition of big companies like EDS and 3com in 2008 and 2009.[8] Throughout the changes taking place in the environment, HP has never left its leadership position in the hardware market including the manufacturing of printers. In 2006[9], HP was able to move ahead of IBM in terms of total revenues and had an annual revenue of USD91.7 billion compared to IBM's USD91.4 billion. Over a third of its revenues now come from services, indicating its adaptation to the environment over the years. Also, HP has expanded to almost every country in the world, indicating its ability to deal with diverse environmental contexts.

HP has a strong focus on innovation with its research arm being located under its office of strategy and technology. By keeping its research initiatives closely connected to its strategy, HP is able to integrate its processes while changes take place in the environment. The office of strategy and technology manages the USD3.6 billion research and development initiatives of HP. Its other functions include managing the technical community of the organization and leading the organization's corporate development efforts. In order to adapt to the environment, HP has taken several courageous decisions such as the merger with Compaq, which was strongly opposed by the son of one of the HP founders.

CONCLUSION

In order to effectively engage with environmental turbulence, organizations must develop information capabilities to monitor the environment. They must also develop the analytical capabilities to make sense of the changes that are taking place. In order to manage uncertainties, organizations must create scenarios that reflect levels of adversity in the environment. For each of these scenarios, organizations must develop detailed plans to evolve their response. They must not only be quick to spot opportunities in the environment and exploit them, but they must also be able to absorb the changes taking place. Organizations must develop synergies between their innovation and business analysis capabilities. They must ensure that these two functions are never in conflict with each other and work towards improving the organization. Organizations must monitor internal behaviour and understand the interdependencies that exist in the environment. By modelling interactions between inputs, processes, and outputs, organizations can craft effective strategic responses to changes in the environment.

NOTES

1. Harrington, R.J., Lemak, D.J., Reed, R., and Kendall, K.W. (2004). 'A Question of Fit: the Links among Environment, Strategy Formulation, and Performance'. *Journal of Business and Management*, 10(1), pp. 15–38.

2. Excerpted from http://www.statebankofindia.com/ on 3 September 2010.

3. Excerpted from http://www.livemint.com/2009/01/25230613/SBI-ICICI-Bank-profits-rise-o.html on 3 September 2010.

4. Excerpted from http://www.forbes.com/2009/05/06/world-reputable-companies-leadership-reputation-table.html on 3 September 2010.

5. Excerpted from http://www.southwest.com/ on 3 September 2010.

6. Excerpted from http://findarticles.com/p/articles/mi_qn4188/is_20040716/ai_n11465633/ on 4 September 2010.

7. Excerpted from http://www.youtube.com/watch?v=EwU9m4oCtRE& on 4 September 2010.

8. Excerpted from http://www.hp.com/hpinfo/execteam/bios/robison.html on 4 September 2010.

9. Excerpted from http://media.corporate-ir.net/media_files/irol/71/71087/pdf/HP_2006AR.pdf on 4 September 2010.

Conclusion

This book has discussed different growth strategies that an organization may employ when they set out to actively expand their business interests. All these strategic tools have been grouped into nine chapters to cover the main areas in which an organization is likely to seek growth.

In view of the growing importance of small and medium enterprises in emerging economies, a separate section has been dedicated to the growth of such organizations.

Today in India, this important sector is something that needs to be studied and nurtured. Our economy is growing fast, and as other countries have proven, this sector can drive much innovation and growth towards the kind of economy we all want to see for India. The good news is that things are happening. Markets are opening in ways and places we've never seen, and today's manager in India is in a good position to capitalize on the growing economy. But there are still many challenges. Hopefully, the information in this book will help readers gain the confidence needed to expand their businesses.

Some challenges to growth are common to all organizations, irrespective of the size of the organization or the strategic tools that are followed. This warranted a separate chapter dedicated to understanding them. But a growing economy is also a beast with many heads, and needs to be dealt with caution. In the present era of market turbulence and heavy competition driven by changes of all kinds, many organizations face decline in performance, slip into the red, or even go bankrupt. A chapter has addressed the concerns of such organizations and suggested some ways to bail themselves out of trouble, with a few illustrations to give an idea of how these problems have been handled by companies we've all heard of and know to be successful by their presence in our everyday lives.

Once an organization has achieved a certain level of success and confidence, riskier propositions such as market disruption can be employed. As was shown in the case of Apple, Steve Jobs and his company had a long plan in place for their eventual iTunes store. In order to make that a success, Apple had to first familiarize customers with the eventual interface. They did this by offering a first and second line of products, which in a sense, were just ways to ease the customer into comfort of use when it came to marketing iTunes, which would pull all other products together into one new industry. At the time, this was a revolutionary strategy.

Moves like these and others outlined in the book depend on external factors, and a stable business environment is essential to launch campaigns with high risk. In unstable environments, organizations have had to work harder and be creative, as we saw with the State Bank of India and Southwest Airlines. These companies thrived in the harshest economic conditions.

All these lessons at all these levels will be useful for those doing business and wanting to grow in India and further afield.

After reading the book, I am sure all managers will find this book a handy reference in their journeys of steering an organization towards a successful, sustainable, and long-term growth trajectory.

Acknowledgements

I have been thinking of writing some books in the areas of my interest for the last couple of years. But this dream always had to be pushed aside, because other priorities took precedence.

It was in a very interesting way that I started writing this book on putting together the various ways in which organizations choose to grow and the importance of growth strategies in satisfying most of the stakeholders. It was during a discussion with Professor Samir Barua, the Director of IIMA that I happened to mention to him that another colleague of mine, a former teacher, Professor M.R. Dixit and I had decided to offer a Management Development Programme on 'Strategies for Growth'. He immediately advised me to think about writing a book on this subject. By that time, IIMA had agreed to publish a series of popular management books to be written by faculty members of IIMA. This happened to be one of topics listed by the publisher as a possible topic of interest to professionals.

Incidentally, I have also been teaching a compulsory course, 'Strategies for Corporate Growth' to the participants of Post Graduate Programme in Management for Executives (PGPX), for the last three years. While searching for an ideal textbook on the subject, I couldn't find one. I always, therefore, was looking for an opportune time to pen down my thoughts, accumulated learning, and insights that I had gained from various articles/research papers and cases, so that the gap for such a textbook could be met.

When I was requested by Professor Barua to write this book, I was very reluctant to do so and was doubtful of completing such a demanding task within the stipulated timeline since I had several other prior commitments. But as it is said, much good work comes out of pressure and stress. This book is probably going to be proof of that. This has been also possible due to very strong support I got from two research scholars at the Institute.

Professor Samir Barua continuously encouraged and inspired me to complete this Herculean task. Chiki Sarkar and Priyanka Sarkar from Random House India played the role of alarm clocks to wake me up whenever I missed the deadline, even if by a day. They also accommodated several delays and requests from my end.

The participants of PGPX of the last three batches (2008, and 2009), at IIMA helped me to sharpen my understanding of growth issues and challenges, during the course of my teaching this subject to them.

I am thankful to many authors of the articles that I have referred to in this book. All of them were glad to know about it and conveyed their best wishes. They are—Professor Philip Kotler, Professor Prashant Kale, Professor Don Hambrick, Professor Vijay Govindarajan, Professor Tarun Khanna, Donald L. Laurie, Derek van Bever, Professor Harbir Singh, Professor Clark Gilbert, Professor Shekhar Chaudhuri, Professor Robert James Harrington, and Dr Elaine M. Cummings.

In spite of all the pain I have gone through during the past several months while writing and editing this book, at the end of the journey I feel extremely happy that I was able to finish this demanding task in time, much to my satisfaction.

A note on IIMA Business Books

The IIM Ahmedabad Business Books bring key issues in management and business to a general audience. With a wealth of information and illustrations from contemporary Indian businesses, these non-academic and user-friendly books from the faculty of IIM Ahmedabad are essential corporate reading. www.iimabooks.com

Would you like to participate

in the IIMA Guru Yatra?

For more details visit

www.iimabooks.com

OTHER BOOKS IN THIS SERIES

INDIA'S BESTSELLING BUSINESS BOOKS SERIES

IIM
AHMEDABAD
BUSINESS BOOKS

STRATEGIES FOR THE FUTURE
Understanding International Business

AJEET N. MATHUR

INDIA'S BESTSELLING BUSINESS BOOKS SERIES

IIM
AHMEDABAD
BUSINESS BOOKS

BUSINESS LAW FOR MANAGERS
Kaleidoscopic Tales

ANURAG K. AGARWAL

INDIA'S BESTSELLING BUSINESS BOOKS SERIES

IIM
AHMEDABAD

DAY TO DAY ECONOMICS

SATISH Y. DEODHAR

INDIA'S BESTSELLING BUSINESS BOOKS SERIES

IIM
AHMEDABAD
BUSINESS BOOKS

CONTRACT TERMS ARE COMMON SENSE

AKHILESHWAR PATHAK